PHalarope Books

PHalarope Books are designed specifically for the amateur naturalist. These volumes represent excellence in natural history publishing. Each book in the PHalarope series is based on a nature course or program at the college or adult education level or is sponsored by a museum or nature center. Each PHalarope Book reflects the author's teaching ability as well as writing ability. Among the books in the series:

The Amateur Naturalist's Handbook
VINSON BROWN

The Amateur Naturalist's Diary
VINSON BROWN

The Wildlife Observer's Guidebook
CHARLES E. ROTH / Massachusetts Audubon Society

A Field Guide to the Familiar:
Learning to Observe the Natural World
GALE LAWRENCE

Nature in the Northwest: An Introduction to
the Natural History and Ecology
of the Northwestern United States
from the Rockies
to the Pacific
SUSAN SCHWARTZ / Photographs by Bob and Ira Spring

At the Sea's Edge: An Introduction to
Coastal Oceanography for the Amateur Naturalist
WILLIAM T. FOX / Illustrated by Clare Walker Leslie

Exploring Tropical Isles and Seas: An Introduction
for the Traveler and Amateur Naturalist
FREDERIC MARTINI

Suburban Wildlife: An Introduction
to the Common Animals of Your
Back Yard and Local Park
RICHARD HEADSTROM

Outdoor Education: A Manual for
Teaching in Nature's Classroom
MICHAEL LINK / Director,
Northwoods Audubon Center, Minnesota

THE ART & DESIGN SERIES

For beginners, students, and working professionals in both fine and commercial arts, these books offer practical how-to introductions to a variety of ideas in contemporary art and design. Each illustrated volume is written by a working artist, a specialist in his or her field, and each concentrates on an individual area—from advertising layout or printmaking to interior design, painting, and cartooning, among others. Each contains information that artists will find useful in the studio, in the classroom, and in the marketplace. Among the books in the series:

Drawing: The Creative Process
SEYMOUR SIMMONS III and MARC S.A. WINER

Nature Drawing: A Tool for Learning
CLARE WALKER LESLIE

Nature Photography: A Guide to
Better Outdoor Pictures
STAN OSOLINSKI

Drawing with Pastels
RON LISTER

Understanding Paintings:
The Elements of Composition
FREDERICK MALINS

Painting and Drawing: Discovering
Your Own Visual Language
ANTHONY TONEY

A Practical Guide for Beginning Painters
THOMAS GRIFFITH

Transparent Watercolor:
Painting Methods and Materials
INESSA DERKATSCH

The Art of Painting Animals:
A Beginning Artist's Guide to the Portrayal
of Domestic Animals, Wildlife, and Birds
FREDRIC SWENEY

CLARE WALKER LESLIE

The Art of
Field Sketching

A SPECTRUM BOOK

PRENTICE-HALL, INC., Englewood Cliffs, New Jersey 07632

Library of Congress Cataloging in Publication Data

Leslie, Clare Walker.
  The art of field sketching.

  (The Art & design series) (PHalarope books)
  "A Spectrum Book."
  Bibliography: p.
  Includes index.
  1. Drawing—Technique.   2. Nature (Aesthetics) in art.
  I. Title.   II. Series.
  NC795.L4   1984   743'.83   83-24461
  ISBN 0-13-047366-9
  ISBN 0-13-047358-8 (pbk.)

THE ART & DESIGN SERIES

This book is available at a special discount when ordered
in bulk quantities. Contact Prentice-Hall, Inc., General
Publishing Division, Special Sales, Englewood Cliffs, N.J. 07632.

1 2 3 4 5 6 7 8 9 10

Editorial/production supervision by Jane Zalenski
Page layout by Diane Heckler-Koromhas
Color insert design by Maria Carella
Color insert photography by James E. Taylor
Cover design by Hal Siegel
Manufacturing buyers: Edward J. Ellis and Frank Grieco

ISBN 0-13-047358-8 {PBK.}

ISBN 0-13-047366-9

PRENTICE-HALL INTERNATIONAL, INC., *London*
PRENTICE-HALL OF AUSTRALIA PTY. LIMITED, *Sydney*
PRENTICE-HALL CANADA INC., *Toronto*
PRENTICE-HALL OF INDIA PRIVATE LIMITED, *New Delhi*
PRENTICE-HALL OF JAPAN, INC., *Tokyo*
PRENTICE-HALL OF SOUTHEAST ASIA PTE. LTD., *Singapore*
WHITEHALL BOOKS LIMITED, *Wellington, New Zealand*
EDITORA PRENTICE-HALL DO BRASIL LTDA., *Rio de Janeiro*

Dedicated to my grandfather, William H. Walker,
and to my father, Robert M. Walker, who both
taught me how to see more carefully.

Contents

Chapter 2

Beginning Exercises and Basic Techniques, 15

Chapter 3

Keeping a Field Journal, 47

Foreword

Many years ago, Ding Darling, the eminent political cartoonist and conservationist, advised a young museum preparatory student, "If you religiously make five or six sketches every day for the next five years you will become an artist." The young man was Maynard Reece, who went on to win the Federal Duck Stamp contest five times and whose canvases of waterfowl and other wildlife now command prices in five figures.

In my youth I would have benefited from similar advice. In my teens I prided myself on detail so fine that it would require a handglass to separate the hairline brush strokes. Like the work of so many other young people who aspire to be wildlife artists, my earlier efforts were lovingly done but far too tight and self-conscious. Then at the age of eighteen, I packed my bags and my brushes and went to art school, the Art Students' League in New York City.

At that elegant old building on 57th Street I enrolled in the class of Kimon Nic-olaides, whose book *The Natural Way to Draw* is still a classic a half century later. Nicolaides taught us to keep our eyes on the model while feeling things out on paper, first tentatively with light delineation, then more positively with stronger confirming lines. To this day I sketch much as I was taught by Nicolaides. Had I enrolled in Bridgeman's class at the League (I couldn't, because his classes were full), I would have learned to draw by blocking in the shapes of things rather than by feeling them out with a fluid line. The schematic drawings in my field guides might not seem to bear this out, but that is another story.

The problem with wild things, particularly birds, is that their movements are so quick and incisive that one must have a photographic memory to arrest an action or a posture in a sketch. As an art student I became accustomed to having a model up there on the stand, holding the same pose for half an hour at a time. But when I made the long ride by subway and elevated train

ROGER TORY PETERSON
Gentoo penguins from the Antarctic.

to the Bronx Zoo as I did once a week, I found that the only birds that would remain as still as the models at the League or the Academy were the great horned owl and the shoe-billed stork. My sketchpads were filled with owls and shoebills, and little else. Eventually I could render either of these birds with only five or six strokes of my pencil.

Although I frequently refer to my 35 millimeter transparencies as a memory jog, I enjoy wildlife photography for its own sake; it is action. Drawing, on the other hand, is cerebral. Whereas a photograph is a record of a fleeting instant, a drawing is a composite of the artist's experience and selectivity. The person who sketches can edit out, delete unnecessary clutter, choose position, and stress basic shape and pattern, unmodified—or modified—by transitory light and shade. The artist has far more options than the photographer, and far more control. This is not a diatribe against photography. I am an obsessive photographer. It is my therapy, but I am fully aware of the differences. Whereas a photograph can have a living immediacy, a good drawing is really more instructive.

One well-known waterfowl artist told me that he often sketched from his 16 millimeter movie film. To do so, he made a short loop of film, two feet or so, joined end to end so that when it went through the projector time after time he could analyze the flight of a duck or a goose. The same wing-strokes would be repeated again and again until he understood exactly what happened. Thus the sketches he drew after studying his film were not unlike those he might have made in the field; they had movement. The action was not frozen as it would have been had he copied a single frame of film.

In January, 1971, when Sir Peter Scott and I were in a Zodiac looking for the rare Auckland teal along the shores of Enderby Island in the Aucklands, we spotted a strange penguin in a small, rocky cave. I leaped ashore with my Nikon; Peter stayed in the Zodiac and took out his sketchpad. As we examined the bird at close range, we debated—was it a Snares penguin or a Fiordland? The two look very much alike. Peter said we would know for sure when we got back to the ship and our reference library. His drawing would tell us. "You will have to wait until you return to Connecticut," he said, "to see your processed photographs."

He was right. His sketch accurately showed the white marks on the cheek and the lack of bare pink skin at the base of the bill. It was a Fiordland penguin, a stray far from its home in New Zealand. Confirming the identification of rare birds by sketching is standard practice among hardcore birders in Britain. The rules are that the sketch must be made on the spot without being influenced by the illustration in a field guide.

I have found that when I am on a guided tour in the Antarctic or on safari in East Africa there is little opportunity to sketch. Too many things are happening too fast. If a cruise director allows us only two hours ashore in a colony of 100,000 penguins, I am more likely to use my camera.

Sketching takes time. Therefore, when traveling I prefer to have my own car or van, and plenty of time to dawdle if there is an opportunity to sketch.

Somehow my fellow tour leader Keith Shackleton has always found time to sketch, and only recently has he invested in a good 35 mm camera. I will be interested to see whether his photography interferes with his sketching or augments it. It is difficult to do both at once. Peter Scott eschews the camera and leaves the photography to his wife, Phillipa, who has a good eye for a picture.

To return to my mention of the field guides: Although the drawings are rather static and patternistic, in comparative profile, suggesting an exhibit of little decoys, they serve a functional purpose which is to teach, to make identification easy. However, a great deal of field sketching went into the preparation of these stylized drawings, more than you might realize. And because my field guide illustrations are what they are, many people think that is the way I always draw birds. They are formal and schematic, not avian portraits in the Audubonesque style or the Fuertes manner; my limited edition prints published by Mill Pond Press are closer to those traditions. Lately my canvases have been going in a more painterly direction, involving environment, third dimensional activity, and movement in space.

But whatever the purpose of a painting or the direction it may take, it should start with numerous sketches. I may make 20 or 30 thumbnail sketches as well as some larger ones before I decide to go ahead. Bob Bateman does the same. Guy Cohleach claims that he might make as many as 100 sketches before he touches brush to canvas. Robert Henri, the great teacher at the Art Students' League, once advised his students to put the bulk of their effort into the planning of a painting. He implied that if the preliminary sketching and basic drawing did not jell, no amount of fiddling and brushwork would save the final painting.

But perhaps you, as a reader of this instructive book by Clare Walker Leslie, have no intention of painting for the galleries; you simply want to sketch. There is no better way to open your eyes to the natural world than to go afield with a sketchpad or notebook. You go beyond mere identification naming things; you begin to understand shape, function, movement, and behavior. Or, if you are esthetically inclined, you may play with line, form, and pattern. Sketching will enhance your awareness of the life forces, and who knows, you might become an artist.

This new book is Clare Walker Leslie's third. Her previous publications are *Nature Drawing: A Tool For Learning* (1980, Prentice-Hall) and *Notes from a Naturalist's Sketchbook* (1981, Houghton Mifflin).

As a teacher, Clare Walker Leslie impresses upon her students the necessity of *getting out* in the field and observing, if only with crude scribbles, the wild and natural behaviors and postures of their subjects. More and more biology students, birdwatchers, and those who just like the outdoors are attending her courses. Usually they are not artists, but wish to sketch quickly and do not know how. Take note of the hot tips she passes on to her students and to you; tips derived in part from such masters as Gunnar Brusewitz of Sweden and John Busby of Britain, with whom she has studied. Even for a lifelong artist such as me, this book is an excellent refresher course.

Roger Tory Peterson

Preface

The art of field sketching is the art of learning to observe and draw nature quickly without worrying about the result. Its methods are simple and its equipment is modest. The sketch enables the viewer to concentrate on recording key features of a subject, its activity and its environment, or simply to record a moment spent being outdoors, watching. Other forms of drawing take too long, demand more skill, and require that more equipment be lugged along. Field sketches can be worked over and refined into finished drawings or paintings later on or simply left as memory jottings. Without the concern for producing a finished work, anyone can do a series of quick sketches while bird watching, hiking along a trail, traveling in a car, or even walking along a city street and, by those simple notations, experience a contact with the natural world that can be extremely fascinating. Much of what I know about nature has come by using sketching to watch, to question, and to learn about a

world that often goes otherwise unnoticed. Wildlife artists and scientists alike refer repeatedly to their field sketches for the bits of information that have been taken directly from the subjects themselves.

Guy Cohleach, a prominent American wildlife artist, commented, "In the field you experience tension, the smell, the mood, the electricity in the air, and the stillness. You capture the feeling and something reminds you of it—a photo or a thumbnail sketch. . . . Usually I just do motion lines to show a rock or limb. When I see it back home, it all comes back."* Because drawing technique and skill are simplified in field sketching, time can be spent in absorbing and studying a situation and in recording it in the most essential forms. Another artist said of field sketching, "If you make a drawing using fifty lines, you make a sketch using ten."

* Patricia Van Gelder, *Wildlife Artists at Work* (New York: Watson-Guptill Publications, 1982), p. 57.

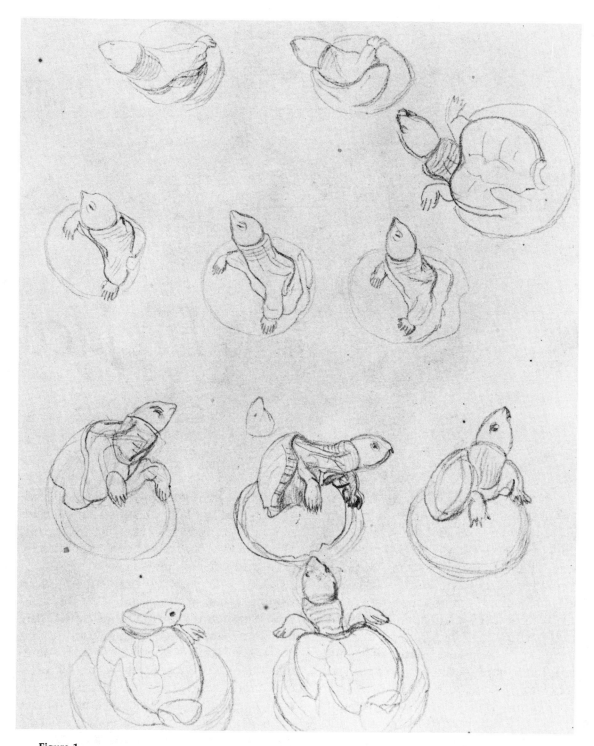

Figure 1
LOUIS AGASSIZ (19th century Swiss scientist)
Turtle Hatching, pencil sketch

Courtesy of the Museum of Comparative Zoology, Harvard University.

Louis Agassiz came to Harvard University in 1847 to take the chair of natural history that was recently established. During his years in America, he did much to promote public as well as scientific interest in the study of natural history. He was often quoted as saying, "Study from nature, not from books." He put great emphasis on learning from nature, and told his students, "If I succeed in teaching you how to observe, my aim will be attained."

This book is intended to give you an idea of what field sketching is all about, for the scientist as well as for the artist. It is intended to give you respect for this technique of drawing as a most valuable method that is *not* inferior to others despite the apparent simplicity of the images. A good sketch can be just as magnificent as a good drawing. The two serve different purposes. It is unfortunate that so many artists do not show their working sketches, fearing that the public will judge their ability accordingly. Historically it has been found that the preliminary sketches of an artist often have been fresher and more spontaneous than the finished work. Although many scientists do not sketch, those who do find that the visual record greatly helps to describe more graphically a particular subject found while in the field. Before the invention of adequate preserving methods, modern photography, or museums to house collected specimens, artist-naturalists often accompanied scientific field trips to make both lengthy drawings and quicker renderings of specimens that could not be brought back.

Although the terms *sketching* and *drawing* blend and overlap, I define *sketching* as that method of quick, gestural drawing that has as its purpose the study of *nature* rather than the study of *drawing*. Drawing, on the other hand, I define as a method intended to produce a finished work of art. Usually a drawing, as opposed to a sketch, has more detail and shows the full technical skill of its creator. A drawing's intention is to explore methods and technique, whereas a sketch's intention is to explore the process of seeing and to gather information. Often a sketch is accompanied by written notes, making it possible for entries to develop into a form of nature diary or journal, as described in Chapter 3. Although I use the term *field sketching* to emphasize outdoor study, I do include several sections on indoor sketching and numerous sketches to broaden the topics and to allow for the natural subjects that are inside our homes, just outside our windows, or in museums, biology labs, or other indoor spaces. Since these terms can be intertwined, ultimately you have to decide for yourself when you are sketching and when you are drawing. Much of it depends on style and purpose. Often, I will have students keep sketches in one book and drawings in another, to keep the two methods separate.

This book provides some fundamental techniques for sketching nature, suggested equipment to use, places and subjects to sketch, some natural history information, and many illustrations that I hope will inspire you to begin your own study. Since outdoor sketching involves going to a variety of locations, the book is organized by habitat rather than by individual subject. The ultimate purpose of this book is to help you look more closely at the natural world

Figure 2
Student sketching at a beaver pond near the base of Mount Washington in the White Mountains of New Hampshire.

and to use sketching as the means. As a student of mine recently said, *"Sketching helps me to get over my fear of drawing. I get so involved looking at something that it no* longer matters to me what the drawing will look like. The experience of being outdoors watching and being so involved is much more valuable than any drawing."

Chapter 1
Equipment

The initial equipment for field sketching should be simple, inexpensive, and portable. Particularly if you are traveling, you want all your sketching things to fit in with the rest of your gear and not take up extra room. On a day trip, be able to carry all you need in a shoulder bag, backpack, or briefcase.

Before you buy costly paper, pens, and pencils, look to see what you already have. People are often inhibited by drawing because they do not know what equipment to use. I have known artists to use the backs of envelopes, scraps of paper, or bits of cardboard if that is all they have at the moment.

Go into an art store and browse. Do not hesitate to ask about paper surfaces and types of drawing tools, and be specific about what your needs are. Use this chapter and the drawing in Figure 1.2 for reference and for suggestions on equipment to have. Each person develops his or her own preferences and, depending upon whether

you are more of an artist or a scientist, whether you will be outdoors or indoors, or whether you will be traveling or staying near home, you will gradually gather the equipment that suits you best. I happen to use an inexpensive black felt-tipped pen a lot—but you may not like it. Remember, though, it is not equipment that will make you draw better but time and experience.

PAPERS

Loose Sheets of Paper

Some people prefer using individual sheets of paper that they fasten to a clipboard and then store later in an indexed portfolio. (See the comments accompanying Figure 7.17.) Good-quality drawing papers can be purchased in loose sheets and cut down to any size. Be sure to ask for drawing—not watercolor or charcoal—paper. Some beginning

Figure 1.1
JOHN SINGER SARGENT (American painter, 1856-1925)
Studies of Turkeys, pencil on paper
Courtesy of the Fogg Art Museum, Harvard University, Cambridge.

Sargent did the sketch in a small notebook, probably one he carried with him regularly, as many artists were accustomed to doing at that time. Perhaps it was a study for a painting, or perhaps this turkey just caught his interest.

Figure 1.2
Recommended equipment to carry when field sketching.
1. Backpack
2. Sketch pad
3. Pencil case
4. Technical drawing pencil (thin lead) or
5. Technical drawing pencil (thick lead)
6. Eraser
7. Pocket knife
8. Extra leads for drawing pencils
9. Several felt-tipped pens
10. Ball-point pen
11. Binoculars
12. Field guide books
13. Magnifying lens
14. Pencil case with a set of ten to fifteen colored pencils
15. Small watercolor set
16. Small brush
17. Small water bottle with a top

Figure 1.3
Clare Walker Leslie sketching, using a 9″ x 12″ spiral-bound pad, a technical pencil, and a field guide to birds for reference while watching a flock of assorted shorebirds along the water's edge.

students prefer to work on the inexpensive but perfectly good duplicator bond paper, which comes in packages of 500 sheets, 8½″ × 11″ in size. I start most of my classes using this versatile paper and find it most useful when working with school students whose budgets are slim. The surface is smooth and so will take both pen and pencil, but because of its low quality it will not take much erasing or water if you are using a watercolor wash.

Drawing Pads

There are many varieties of drawing pads. Some have paper with a rough surface, best for holding watercolor or pastels. Some have very smooth surfaces, for holding ink and hard pencil or for watercolor used in the dry brush method. Spiral-bound pads are better than glue-bound pads because the pages can be folded back and will still stay in the pad. But the glue-bound pads often seem to have the better-quality papers.

Choose a smooth-surfaced, medium-weight paper. Grainy paper will cause a more textured drawing and a pencil line that can smudge unless sprayed with fixative. The thin papers will not take heavy lines well, can tear with erasing, and can

blur ink lines. Sizes of papers vary greatly, but for most common use a 9″ × 12″ pad, which can be easily held while standing, still allows for a full page of sketches. A 5″ × 8″ pad is good when traveling and can be carried easily in a pocket. And an 11″ × 14″ pad works well if you are sketching at a table.

Field Journal

A full description of the field journal and its uses can be found in Chapter 3. If you want to begin a seasonal sketch journal or nature diary, buy a hardbound drawing book. It gives a sense of permanence to your recordings and can be set up so that you can use it through one full year or through the full course of an expedition. It also holds up well if carried outdoors a great deal. Keep a spiral pad for your finished drawings and for studies in drawing technique.

Hardbound drawing books are available in most art or stationery stores. Although they come in various sizes, the 8″ × 11″ is often most suitable, since it fits well into a day pack yet is still large enough for good-sized sketches. Some students do prefer the 6″ × 9″ books (as in Figure 1.4) or the larger 11″ × 14″ ones. Be aware of paper quality, as some hardbound books have

Figure 1.4
Sketches drawn by a student while traveling in Washington. These were entered in a 6″ x 9″ hardbound sketchbook with a felt-tipped pen and pencil for shading. On returning, the student noted how the sketches had made her observe and remember the landscape much more specifically.

low-grade bond paper and may cause ink sketches to bleed through to the reverse side. Strathmore makes a hardbound book with a very serviceable, quality paper. In most art stores, the bond paper type of drawing book comes with a black cover. The books with the red covers contain higher-quality paper and are much more expensive.

SKETCHING TOOLS

It is best to use either pencil or pen when field sketching. Charcoal, pastels, or other types of drawing tools smudge and must be sprayed. Clarity of image can blur and the process of sketching can become labored. Save those tools for other drawing methods in which any medium may be used.

Pencils

Pencils come either in the usual wooden form or as leads contained in mechanical holders. A technical pencil is useful in the field because the lead can be retracted so that it does not break in carrying. Indoors, I prefer the lead pencil because the graphite quality is better in my opinion, and one can get a more varied edge on the lead point. Technical pencils can be sharpened with a mechanical sharpener, and those with very thin leads need not be sharpened at all—a distinct advantage when you need to sketch continuously and do not want a dull point.

Leads for both types of pencils come in a range of weights. A 6H is very hard and is mostly used to sketch out a drawing that will be inked over or for drawing on tracing paper. A 6B is very soft and will smudge but allows for a more colorful series of tones. Generally I use an HB or 2B pencil when drawing plants and animals and a 3B, 4B, or 5B when drawing landscapes. The standard number 2 yellow writing pencil is perfectly adequate, although it does not have the better-quality graphite of the artists' pencils.

Erasers Some technical pencils have erasers attached. Othewise, a white drafting plastic eraser made by Koh-i-noor or Faber Castel works best for careful drawings as well as for quick sketches. The common pink eraser is fine, although it can smear and tear the paper. Some students prefer the kneaded rubber erasers. Instead of rubbing out the image with them, you can pick or twist it off the paper's surface. The art gum erasers, while good for some purposes, crumble and do not erase small lines well. Whatever you use, you need to keep it handy and to make sure you don't smear your image when you erasing.

Pencil sharpeners While the mechanical pencils take their own type of sharpener, wooden pencils can be sharpened with a pocketknife, sandpaper, X-acto blade, or some sort of portable pencil sharpener.

Pen and Ink

It really is your personal preference whether you use pen more than pencil. Both have their own qualities. Use both and

Figure 1.5
This 3B pencil sketch of a wolf was one of several sketches done on a trip to draw the northern hemisphere mammals on display at Harvard's Museum of Comparative Zoology. No more than ten minutes were spent sketching as I stood with my pad awkwardly propped up while numerous school children were curious to see what I was doing.

see which you like better and when. And use them together, as in Figure 7.15. When using pen I find that my lines are more careful, more scientifically diagrammatic, though less varied in tone and color and perhaps even less artistic. I do use pen and ink a great deal in the field because pencil can be difficult to get crisp images with, and I do a lot of writing beside the sketches, which works better with a pen for me. If I am sketching a landscape or doing more finished drawings of animals, I will use pencil. Some students sketch in pencil and write their field notes in pen. Some ink over their initial pencil sketches later. Again, it depends on what sort of sketch you wish to produce.

I seldom carry my technical drawing pens, fountain pens, or other quill pens outdoors. Aside from their being expensive to replace if lost, they are finicky. They can clog, bleed ink, dry up, or congeal with the cold. A felt-tipped pen does not produce as fine a quality of line or as good an ink, but it is reliable. Reliability in field sketching is key. You do not want your equipment to get in the way of your recording an experience. Since the ink of the felt tip is not permanent, a wash-over of tones with a wet finger or watercolor brush can result in what I call the "poor person's watercolor" (see Figure 7.23).

Art stores now carry a variety of permanent ink felt-tipped markers in a number

Figure 1.6
This page was done with a felt-tipped pen in a 6″ x 9″ spiral pad I often carry with me. I drew from the car window, pausing briefly for a quiet moment in an otherwise busy day.

Figure 1.7
JOHN BUSBY (British artist/naturalist)
Fountain pen sketch of a young otter.

of widths and colors. Although nice to use for a change, their lines can blur, even through to the other side of the paper.

Another useful item to have is a ball-point pen, either blue or black. In the rain, it is the only tool that will not blur and yet is dark enough to be legible. It is also something you are more likely to be carrying with you in a pocket or backpack than a more expensive pen. There are numerous wildlife artists, such as Robert Bateman of Canada, who prefer ball-point pens to other tools when sketching outdoors.

Color Tools and Watercolor Washes

One of the biggest drawbacks to drawing in general is the lack of color. In the field, one doesn't usually have time to set up a water-color painting and rarely an oil or acrylic study. But there are many quick ways to add color to field sketches, enough so that if it is referred to later, the color information will be useful. Since there is so much wonderful color in nature it is a pleasant change to leave the grays and blacks of pencil and pen for a bit of blue, orange, green, and brown.

Colored felt-tipped pens and markers   There is a wide number of colored felt-tipped pens that come in sets or individually. Although the colors tend to be gaudy, they are nice to use for quick and colorful sketching. Since most of them are water soluable, you can add a wet brush to them to get some water-color effects as well. The larger permanent ink markers can be interesting to try when sketching landscapes where broad areas of tone are needed and only rather abstract forms are being defined. Again, be willing to experiment.

Crayons   Crayons can be used for additions of color to a sketch. They do not mix well and getting detail can be difficult. But their brilliance and their wide range of colors at an inexpensive price make them good to use in the classroom. They are particularly effective for a landscape that describes the abstract color shapes of a scene rather than its details.

Colored Pencils   Colored pencils are perhaps the best color tool for field sketching. They can be used like a pencil and yet their broad range of colors allows for a good amount of tonal buildup. Colored pencil can be added to a pencil sketch, as in Figure 1.8, or to a pen and ink sketch, as in Figure 7.4. They carry well when it's important to have a limited amount of equipment. And they can be erased. Although watercolor is wonderful to use outdoors, it does mean carrying along more things and is more complicated to work with than are colored pencils. There has been a recent increase of interest in colored pencil drawings in both scientific illustration and in graphic art, and books on its use are appearing on the market.

Two brands that I use are the Berol Prismacolor and the Venus Spectracolor because they blend well and their color range is broad. Some other brands produce a harder line and do not blend as well. Caron d'Arche markets a set of colored pencils that will turn into a watercolor wash when a wet brush is applied. I carry a set of thirty-five pencils with me in a plastic case as part of my regular equipment.

Figure 1.8
This study using fountain pen with colored pencil was done during a field
drawing class at the beach. It demonstrates how to structure a simple landscape
composition that has artistic design elements, and also conveys an awareness
of the natural history within the habitat.

Watercolor The many varied ways of using watercolor are much too lengthy a subject to discuss in any detail in this book. The method I use and find most appropriate for field study work is more in the manner of the British tradition where a fairly dry brush is used on a heavy piece of smooth-surfaced paper. (I use a quality bristol paper or illustration board more than I use watercolor paper.) The purpose for color is to illustrate a subject, so it is best to be as accurate with your brush strokes as possible. I have learned this method by studying the works of such artists as Beatrix Potter, the British artist, naturalist, and writer of the Peter Rabbit books; Gunnar Brusewitz, the Swedish artist and naturalist represented in this book; John Busby, the British artist represented here; Arthur Singer, whose illustrations in *The Birds of North America* are most useful when learning to draw birds; and the numerous watercolor illustrations found predominantly in children's books.

I lay down a fairly detailed pencil sketch before I apply any color, then go back and add more pencil or pen if need be. However, do not take more than forty-five minutes on a watercolor sketch to keep the impression fresh and unmuddied. So often I have found that if I stop and go on with another study, the first looks tight and forced and the second looks freer and more effectively rendered. Your best teacher can be your own drawings and the process you go through while doing them.

If you are a beginner, ask your art store for a decent set of watercolors for roughly ten dollars and be sure to get two or three fairly decent brushes. For detail work, get a size 5; for general laying in of tones, get a size 12. Brushes come larger and smaller, with pointed as well as flat ends. Winsor and Newton now sells a *Sketcher's Water Colour Pocket Box* (see Figure 1.2) that is only 4" × 2½" and can easily fit into any pouch or backpack. Be sure to carry a water bottle for rinsing brushes.

Figure 1.9
GUNNAR BRUSEWITZ (contemporary Swedish artist/naturalist)
Watercolor study of a tree in winter.
Speaking of his technique, Brusewitz says, "My 'method' is very simple: just sitting on a stone or a stump with my sketchbook, making drawings from nature with my pencils. That's in fact all. Back in my studio, I start with brushes and watercolors . . . I don't like to overdo my sketches. I like them fresh and not too detailed and perfect . . . I always have a small pocket sketchbook with me when I am outdoors. If I find anything interesting, I stop for a very rough pencil sketch, and if it still interests me when I am back in my studio I try to make something out of it." [Personal communications, August and December, 1982.]

Figure 1.10
JOHN BUSBY (Contemporary British artist/
naturalist)
Great tit and robin sketches.
Charcoal pencil with color wash tones.
With just a few strokes, Busby is able to
define the basic posture and shape of
these birds. This has come from many
years of continuous observation and
drawing.

I do not recomend using acrylic or oil in sketching because a fair amount of equipment is required and it can take longer to complete a work.

OTHER USEFUL EQUIPMENT

Drawing Board

If you want to sketch on loose sheets of paper, clip them to a heavy cardboard (I use 8½″ × 11″ mat board for my beginning students) or to a piece of masonite. Art stores supply masonite drawing boards of varying sizes that are very nicely made and are useful for carrying outdoors. I use an 18″ × 19″ masonite board (propped up to a 45° angle) when drawing indoors and a 15″ × 16″ masonite board when carrying along an assortment of paper to sketch outdoors.

Clips

Paper clips, rubber bands, or other clasps are convenient to hold paper down when the wind is blowing or to mark your place in a journal.

Six-inch Ruler

A 6″ ruler can be useful for measuring proportions of a plant or animal when size is important for identification.

Carrying Cases

Inexpensive zippered pencil cases hold an assortment of pens, pencils, erasers, and sharpeners. They can be purchased at any art or stationery store. Larger boxes can be cumbersome, and the plastic case forces you to carry only the essentials.

Carrying Bag or Day Pack

Camping supply stores are well equipped with satchels, bags, and cases to suit campers' every need. I use a small day pack for my sketching gear, since it is large enough to carry the basics and no more.

Binoculars and Hand Lens

Binoculars are indispensible if you are sketching birds, animals, and even landscapes at any distance. The size most commonly used has a maginification of 7 and a diameter of field vision measuring 35, which are the figures represented in the formula that describes the various types of binoculars. The most popular types that bird-watchers carry are 7 × 35 or 8 × 40. The brands, however, greatly vary in price and quality. A small hand lens or magnifying glass is handy when looking at small parts of plants, insects, or anything with fine detail.

Camera

Many wildlife artists become skilled photographers so that they have their own pictures as reference material, with such details as coloration, individual features of an animal or plant, or the composition of a landscape. If I am having difficulty isolating a particular landscape to sketch, I will sometimes look through my camera to help frame a scene with the most interesting compositional elements.

But a camera cannot be selective, nor can it describe more than what the lens sees. A sketch, on the other hand, can interpret, can combine several images into one, and does not need to wait for laboratory development. Use your own photographs in conjunction with field sketches, other people's photographs, skinned specimens, and, of course, with the subject itself. Most wildlife artists refer to photographs at one point or another in their work, and, in fact, most have extensive photo files coded according to species or habitat. But they will tell you that it has been the hours in the field observing the animals directly that has given them the best knowledge of their subjects. A good eye can usually spot those paintings which have been done from photographs and not from the living model.

American novelist Eudora Welty made a fine point about her use of a camera, much as the artist would: "My little inexpensive Kodak was a hand-held auxiliary of my wanting to know. I could bring home whatever I saw and see it again as if slowed down. A snapshot caught a moment to keep, yet a moment that of itself showed life running."* So it can be with sketching.

A word of caution, though: If you are publishing your drawings and their subject has been taken from a photograph, make certain you do not directly copy pose or composition without permission from the photographer because copyright laws are strict on this matter.

Plastic Bags or Bottles

Plastic bags of varying sizes can be large enough to protect you or your equipment in a sudden downpour or can be used to sit on. Small bags can hold small specimens for later identification or for more detailed drawing once back home. Bottles are good for any fragile items such as bones, egg cases, and seed pods or for temporarily catching insects to be sketched more closely.

Field Guide Books and Further References

Limit what you take into the field. At most, bring along one bird- and one plant-identification guide. The two I use most often are Chandler S. Robbin's *A Guide to Field Identification of Birds of North America* and Roger Tory Peterson's *A Field Guide to Wildflowers*. But, the best thing to do is to make your sketches descriptive enough to work out

* *The Boston Globe*, April 29, 1983.

identification later when you're back home. It wastes precious observation time to be riffling through books instead of observing and memorizing the subject at hand. (See Figure 6.18 for an example of diagnostic sketches done without a guide book.)

Listed in the bibliography are a number of other guides that I have found helpful. Go to the library and look through their nature/natural science section, or browse in a local bookstore. Often some of the best natural history books are in the children's sections of libraries and bookstores. Since those who study natural history have done so mostly on their own, you will find that much learning will occur by developing your own paths of interests. It does help to find out what local environmental organizations are doing in the way of field trips, courses, and other programs. Ask at your library or local Chamber of Commerce. Increasingly, colleges are opening their biology departments to field study courses, and there are growing opportunities to go on natural history study trips with local, state, national, and international organizations.

Appropriate Clothing

Since, by definition, most field sketching is done outdoors, learn to dress for the weather. You may be out thirty minutes or all day. It is difficult to sketch when the fingers are too cold to hold the pencil. And yet, some of the most exciting sketching can be done under the worst conditions, when animals are more active or the light on a landscape is more dramatic. Wear fingerless gloves, blow warm air frequently onto your hands, keep moving, and bring along a warm drink. Be sure to have along a wool hat, extra sweaters, and so on.

For the hot days, bring along dark glasses to take the glare off the white paper, cool clothing, and a thermos of water and a snack. If too hot, find a tree to sit under, but be aware of the shadows and lights coming

Figure 1.11
Student sketching a tree felled and then chewed by a beaver in the White Mountains of New Hampshire. As this was November and quite chilly, we were all dressed warmly and did not sketch long. Notice that the student is using a hardbound sketchbook and an ordinary pencil.

through form the waving leaves which can dapple your drawing page. Some of my most memorable sketching times have been in the worst weather, when rain has splattered my paper and wind has blown the hair into my eyes. One time I was out on a desolate and rainswept beach when up came a gyrfalcon flying over the dunes after a flock of shorebirds. I would not have missed the chance to sketch despite the wet and chill.

Folding Camp Stool, Waterproof Pillow, or Foam Pad

I do not carry things to sit on, since I find them just one more item to hold. But, if you are to be in one place for a while, they can be most practical. I usually sketch standing or sitting on my jacket or on a rock.

A Word On Collecting

Do not pick, collect, or cut any specimens unless you know it is permitted. Many private or public areas have specific rules on this subject. Do not pick any wildflowers unless you are sure they are abundant. Federal laws exist against collecting birds' eggs and nests, and road kills. If you do find a dead animal, keep it only temporarily, and keep it wrapped in a bag in the refrigerator or freezer to maintain the body's freshness, until you have drawn it (see the chickadee studies in Figure 4.4). Then dispose of it properly.

Curiosity

Perhaps the most important thing to have is a desire to be outdoors and to observe with true curiosity both the large and the small happenings of the natural world, gradually evolving your own system of learning. The best form of education is that which comes from one's own self-derived curiosity. I am self-taught in this area of drawing and natural history study, as there simply are no courses nearby or teachers from whom I can learn. You get bits of knowledge here and there and from years of accumulated looking, reading, asking questions (sometimes foolish), and finding those like-minded people who can share with you the adventures of exploring outdoors.

When looking at nature, begin formulating questions so that you can go beyond learning just the names of things. Try to devise questions which will help you look more closely at behavior, patterns of activity in animals, and habitat conditions in plants and landscapes. Ask yourself, for example, "How does the spider make its web?" or "Why might that sparrow be singing there?" so that you can learn something *about* the creature, beyond a mere portrait, while you are sketching it. Recognize that there may not always be answers to your questions, but learning how to formulate good questions can greatly help your powers of observation as well as your ability to record what you sketch.

In 1976, I was fortunate enough to attend a course with the British wildlife artist and naturalist Dr. Eric Ennion (whose sketches can be seen in Figures 2.15 and 6.26). At 76, he was still observing new things about the animals he sketched out in the meadows and woodlands near his home. He taught me to draw animals as I saw them and not as mere subjects or pretty pictures. He told me that a drawing should tell the truth about an animal. He would say, "When you are not sure what an animal looks like, don't make it up; go back and look at the animal again, again, and then again." Dr. Ennion is quoted as saying:

> Whoever seeks to do so must, first, train himself to observe and set down what he saw at once and quickly; . . . one needs real knowledge of the birds and beasts one paints and of the shifting scene around them—a naturalist, like the elephant's child, must have insatiable curiosity.*

* John Busby, *The Living Birds of Eric Ennion* (London: Victor Gollancz, 1982), pp. 114 and 118.

Figure 1.12
TERENCE SHORTT (Chief artist of the Royal Ontario Museum, Emeritus)
Pencil studies of a black lemur drawn in Madagascar.
Shortt is one of Canada's outstanding bird artists. He has spent a lifetime studying, traveling, and painting animals. His ability to get essential forms with minimal lines and shading is the skill of an accomplished artist. Compare his method of shading with Figure 1.6, which was done in pen.

Chapter **2**

Beginning Exercises & Basic Techniques

It is important to recognize right away that in sketching you are essentially note-taking and that in drawing you are aiming to produce a finished product. Don't worry if the sketch seems "wrong"; just go on and do another, refining and refining your observation as it gets better. In sketching, it is best to look less at the paper and more at the object until you have firm in your mind's eye its essential shape, movement, and key features. Then, you can begin to hone in on a more finished study, if you wish.

Larry McQueen, an ornithological artist from Oregon, noted several important points about field sketching:

> It has taken me a long time to accept the notion that a field sketch need not be a thing of beauty to convey the relevant information. There is such a heritage of beautiful field sketches (Fuertes, Sutton, T.M. Shortt, etc.) that we do tend to uphold as models and accept anything less

with dissatisfied resignation, if at all. A thing of beauty is a worthy goal, but it should not be held with such high regard, that it interferes with the real purpose of a field sketch; that is something the artist uses to enhance his (or her) understanding of the subject and increase his (or her) facility in visual note-taking. I have to continually remind myself of this."*

To first get a sense of what field sketching is about, look through this book, randomly reading bits and looking at the illustrations until you are inspired enough to try it yourself. The illustrations have been carefully chosen to be used as a base for exercises you are to do for yourself, depending upon your own interests, the area where you live, and the subjects you want to observe. Begin by going through the following exercises, in order, preferably indoors or in a quiet place outdoors where

* Personal correspondence, January 10, 1983.

you will have at least half an hour of undisturbed time. Have patience with yourself, allowing time to experiment, throw away, and "waste" paper. This is not a course that will take one month to master but many months and many seasons.

BEGINNING EXERCISES

Although called *beginning*, these exercises are used by artists on all skill levels and are used as the principal methods when sketch-ing or drawing both outdoors and indoors. They may be used individually or in sequence. But here it is recommended that you do them all and in the order described.

Exerise 1
CHOOSING WHAT TO DRAW

Never draw anything that doesn't interest you, or your drawing will reflect your attitude. It is preferable for these exercises that you choose something inanimate, fairly simple in form, and not particularly large. If you choose a plant or tree branch, draw only as much as eight inches of

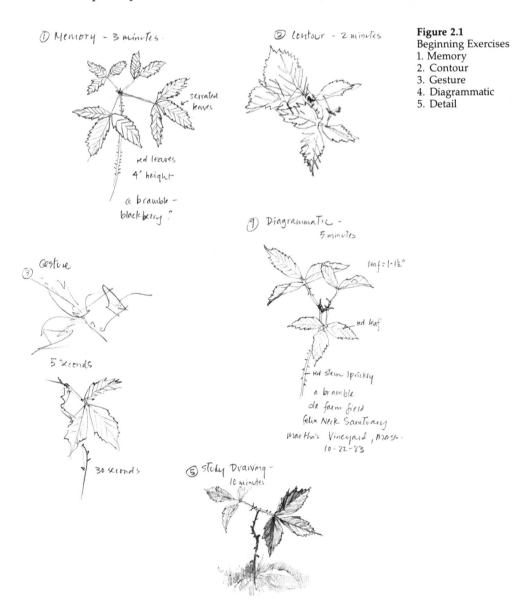

Figure 2.1
Beginning Exercises
1. Memory
2. Contour
3. Gesture
4. Diagrammatic
5. Detail

the specimen. If you try drawing more, you will find yourself repeating forms and spending too much time filling your page. It can be something from the outdoors such as a seed pod or an interesting leaf, or it can be something from indoors such as a collected shell or even a piece of fruit from the refrigerator.

Exercise 2
OBSERVATION

Always spend a few minutes looking carefully at your object, clearing your mind of the distractions you have just come from. Turn it around; analyze its shape from various positions, asking yourself questions such as why it was formed this way, how it grew, where it came from; observe its details in features, texture, and color. Training the eye to see is as important as training the hand to draw.

Exercise 3
MEMORY SKETCH

Many wildlife artists use the memory sketch technique in the field. British wildlife artist Eric Ennion used to say, "If you have a choice between sketching and watching, watch and jot down what you remember later on after the animal has gone and you have gathered an assortment of accumulated, memory images." Take just a minute or so to memorize four or five key features that will enable you to fairly accurately re-create your object on paper. (Put the object out of sight so that you won't be tempted to sneak a glance at it.) Then, do a simple line drawing, marking down all the things about it you have recalled. Add written notes about size, color, or other information, if you wish. After several minutes, when you feel you have drawn enough, take out your object and look to see what you remembered and what you did not. I am often amazed at how little I really do notice. Draw it again from memory, if you have the time, repeating the exercise.

Memory sketching is an important technique to develop because it means you can always be looking for subjects to draw whether you have

paper and pencil with you or not. The red squirrel and birds at the feeder in Figure 4.3 were sketched by a combination of memory and gesture. The birds in the field sketch in Figure 4.30 were sketched from memory as soon as they moved away from me. And Figure 7.24 was done fully from memory by British artist John Busby after he returned from a day watching and sketching seabirds on the cliffs near his home in Scotland. Although he had his sketches laid out beside him, he used them only for occasional reference. Roger Tory Peterson, the well-known American bird artist, remarked to me that "you must have a very good memory, nearly photographic, in fact, to describe exactly all you saw while outdoors."

Exercise 4
CONTOUR OR CONTINUOUS
LINE SKETCH

This time, look only at the object and not at your paper. Place the object far enough away from the paper so that you will not be tempted to look at your sketch while you draw (see the students drawing this exercise, in Figure 2.2). Place your pencil on the page and do not lift it the entire time while your eye wanders slowly and carefully over the object's entire contour. By contour, I mean not just the outline, but all the ins and outs, as though your pencil were an ant or your finger investigating the entire surface of the form. If out at an end of one direction, just turn and draw back again without lifting up the pencil. Take about three minutes, looking thoroughly and transcribing what you see directly with your hand. Look at Figures 2.1 and 2.2.

The drawing may make you laugh. It will not resemble the object as you would draw it otherwise, but, if you look carefully, your lines will show close references to curves, angles, and the general features of the object. There may even be some surprising likenesses expressed, as in Figure 2.3, which was done by a student who had never drawn before. I have often found some of the best observing and line use done by students in this exercise. Sometimes I will suggest to advanced students that they use contour

Figure 2.2
College students in an interdisciplinary art and biology course doing an exercise of drawing nature outdoors by using the contour drawing technique.

drawing when first warming up for a drawing session. It loosens the hand and gets one relying on the eyes, and not solely the brain, for information to record. In the field, I will do contour drawings when an animal is moving fast and I wish to get a series of its changing positions without looking down at my paper and, thus, losing valuable observing moments. Figures 2.3 and 4.23 were done by a combination of contour and gesture sketching.

Exercise 5
QUICK GESTURE SKETCH

Gesture sketching is the most important method to use when drawing outdoors. It is the term used for any sketching that is done rapidly. Whereas in contour drawing you look slowly and in detail, the gesture sketch gets you to look

quickly, energetically, and at the whole form all at once. Lines are drawn loosely, without hesitation, using the full motion of the arm, and often produce a scribbly image, as in the third example of Figure 2.1, or Figure 6.8. Look at your object and your paper simultaneously. Do not pause to judge or erase; just draw over and go on. These sketches can take from three seconds to one minute to do. Erasing can be done later when you are ready to develop a study to a more finished degree. Do not bother with much shading, if any at all.

Gesture sketching was done a great deal by the master draftsmen throughout the history of art. Look at the sketches of Michelangelo, Rembrandt, Delacroix, Van Gogh, Ingres, Cézanne, Picasso, Tiepolo, or Degas for methods in sketching. It is always advisable to look at the works of the masters, for there you will find examples of the best in drawing technique. (See the Bibliography for several recommended texts on drawing technique.)

In this exercise, hold your pencil lightly. Even stand up if your object is placed on the table or on the ground. Try drawing with the opposite hand. Try using a brush with one color ink or paint or a large felt-tipped pen. Try anything to loosen your strokes and your hand and to speed along your seeing/recording connection.

Time yourself. Do a fast sketch in just three seconds. (I time students very exactly with these initial exercises.) Then turn your object around and do another sketch in five seconds. Do not worry if you get nothing more than three strokes or only part of the object. Just pretend that it is alive and continuously moving. Next, increase to thirty seconds and then to one minute. Use an egg timer so you will not be tempted to run over. Do several pages of fast sketches averaging about 6" in size. In art schools, these warm-up gestures begin just about all figure drawing sessions and are considered part of an artist's repertoire. It is important not to fuss over a sketch but to go on, to keep learning from the object and not from the drawing. When sketching outdoors, I feel I am always "buying time," as I refer to it, since I never know when an animal is going to vanish or how long I can stay in one spot.

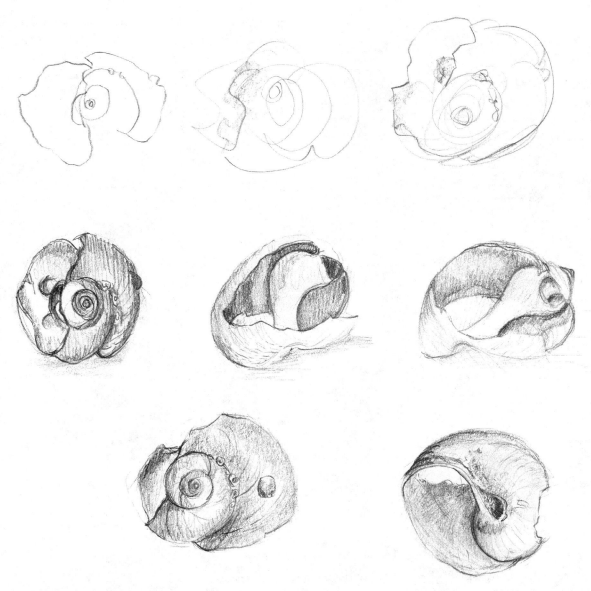

Figure 2.3
A student's use of the contour method combined with gesture as a warm-up
exericse before drawing a shell. This also illustrates a worthwhile exercise—that
of drawing something from different positions in order to gain better
knowledge of the whole form.

Exercise 6
DIAGRAMMATIC DRAWING

Spend no more than five minutes doing a simple line drawing of the object, identifying it in the manner that a field guide would. (A helpful reference for this style of drawing is Roger Tory Peterson's A Field Guide to Wildflowers *or any other plant guide in which a solid line drawing appears.) Add written notes to supplement your observations. (See example 4 in Figure 2.1.) Do not shade or be overly technical in your drawing style. This method does not intend that you produce a drawing as much as a visual record principally for identification purposes. (See Figures 6.6 or 6.18 as examples.)*

Exercise 7
EXPERIMENTING WITH THE
PENCIL LINE

Now it is time to learn the range of marks, lines, tones, and the various symbols your pencil can make, as shown in Figure 2.5. I compare the pencil to the voice. Both can be used in a monoto- *nous way or with a lot of color and variation. Often the most interesting drawings are those in which a range of pencil strokes and color tones have been used. Take a piece of paper and try using your pencil in as many ways as you can. Do this same exercise with pen, colored pencil, crayon, or watercolor.*

Figure 2.4
Experiment with pencil lines, tonal ranges, and the various effects created by using different tools. Learn how your equipment can work for you.

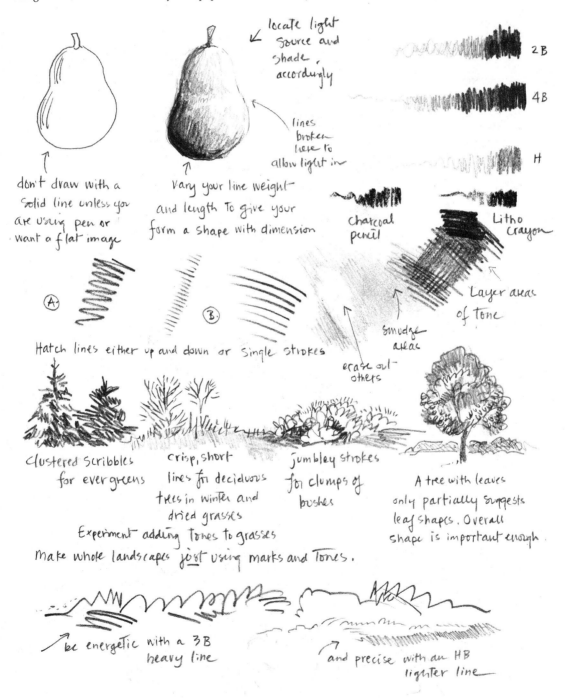

Exercise 8
THE STUDY DRAWING

You may have suitable conditions outdoors for sitting a while and completing a fifteen minute or even a one hour drawing. This is where the terms sketching *and* drawing *merge. If definitions concern you, then define for yourself when you feel one has become the other. In this case, do a drawing so that you can experience for yourself what it is like to set out with the purpose of finishing a piece that will push you to your best skill level thus far. If you are a beginning draftsperson, look at Figure 2.6 for suggested steps to follow.*

If you are not certain whether you have finished, leave your drawing for a while; tape it on the wall or put it up to a mirror to reverse the image for a fresh look. Sometimes I even photostat drawings before finally finishing them to get yet another view on them. It is best when in doubt to leave a drawing for a while. You can always go back and do more work but it is difficult to undo what has been overworked.

Exercise 9
DRAWING AS MEDITATION

To keep yourself from becoming too analytical with drawing technique or too investigative with nature study, it can be a regenerative shift to do an exercise modified from those that Frederick Franck describes in his book The Zen of Seeing: Seeing/Drawing as Meditation. *Take your sketch pad and pencil (or pen) and go outdoors to a place where you can find stillness and no human distractions. Sit quietly, or walk slowly, being fully aware of everything around you. Listen, breathe deeply, let your mind flow easily. When something catches your eye, sketch it with the single thought of getting to know it and only it. Perhaps hardly look at your paper. Add any commentary you wish. Do not hurry. Look at Franck's drawing in Figure 2.5 which is a page taken from his other book of similar philosophy entitled* Art as the Way. *You might want to read, inconjunction, some Thoreau, Annie Dillard, William Wordsworth, American Indian or Oriental writings, or other works by the vari-*

Figure 2.5
FREDERICK FRANCK (artist from New York)
A page from *Art as the Way*, by Frederick Franck. (New York: The Crossroad Publishing Company, 1981, p. 38.)
Reproduced courtesy of the publisher and Frederick Franck.

Dr. Franck is a professional artist, writer, musician, and philosopher who has given numerous workshops on seeing/drawing as meditation. During one workshop, he made the comment, "Studying nature gets us beyond ourselves and into the larger world of more universal images." [April 1983]

During that flash "the artist" died a sudden death and was no more. But the image-maker survived him, was more alive than ever. I started to draw, furiously, as if it were a matter of life and death. For in that flash I had retrieved the original impulse that long ago made me start painting: to SEE, to really see this wondrous world before I die, to make it my own...

of whom are listed in the Bibliography of this book.

CHECKLIST OF TECHNIQUES TO USE WHEN SKETCHING ANY SUBJECT

1. *Be observant of page layout when placing your sketches.* Do not cramp small sketches into one corner and leave the rest of the page empty. Do not run off the paper. Do not write untidy notes beside careful sketches. Although these are rough sketches, it takes only a moment to think about where your image should go and how will it fit with the others. You may wish to look at the sketches later or use them in further study. It can be unfortunate to get home only to find valuable notes indecipherable, pages torn, or images too smudged to read.

2. *Angle your paper.* Hold your drawing pad at an *angle* so that you can see your

Figure 2.6
Suggestions for sketching an inanimate object.

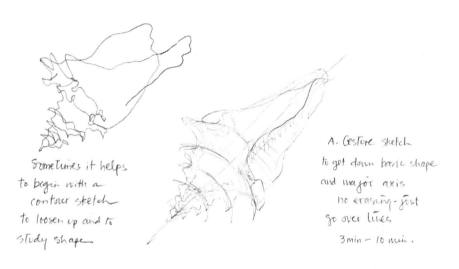

Sometimes it helps to begin with a contour sketch to loosen up and to study shape

A. Gesture sketch to get down basic shape and major axis no erasing - just go over lines

3 min - 10 min.

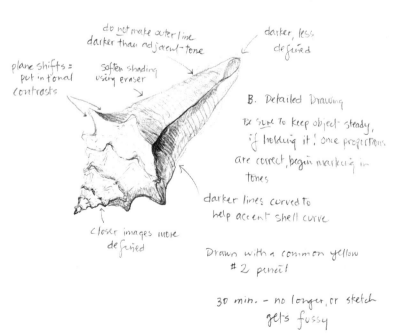

do not make outer line darker than adjacent tone

plane shifts = put in tonal contrasts

Soften shading using eraser

darker, less defined

B. Detailed Drawing
Be sure to keep object steady, if holding it! Once proportions are correct, begin marking in tones

darker lines curved to help accent shell curve

closer images more defined

Drawn with a common yellow #2 pencil

30 min. - no longer, or sketch gets fussy

page and your subject simultaneously and not have to continually shift your vision or get a crick in the neck from bending over a flat drawing surface.

3. *Match pencil lead or ink tool with grade of paper.* Sometimes students smudge their sketches, unable to get clean lines, or discover their ink drawings "bleed" into the paper on the reverse side. This will happen if they are not careful to match the weight of the drawing tool with the surface texture of the paper. If a paper is textured, it needs a *sharpened* pencil and one that is on the hard side, such as an H or HB. A 2B, 3B, or 4B will smear if pressed heavily onto rough paper or if not kept sharp. A thick paper will cause ink to blur and to bleed. Quality drawings in both pen and ink and even watercolor should be done on a smooth-surfaced bristol-type paper or on illustration board.

If your hand is smudging your drawings, begin on a part of the page farthest away from your drawing hand and work in that direction. Try also to have only the edge of your palm on the paper.

4. *See geometric shapes within forms before seeing detail.* It is easiser to get proportions correct when you are working with more than just outline. Sketch *into* the form of the body, or *across* the parts of the plant, or *through* the abstract shapes of the landscape. It is easier to get proportions correct when working within smaller areas than with the form as a whole. Often, I will first mark down the principal line of movement by drawing in the major axis of a plant stem or tree trunk, or the backbone curve of a bird or other animal. Then I build around that line. In Figure 2.6, that line has been drawn along the axis of the shell. In Figure 2.12, a line determines the posture of each bird.

5. *Continuously check proportions.* In sketching natural forms, it is essential that the sizes of the various parts within the

Figure 2.7
Studies of foreshortening in a poinsettia plant.

Figure 2.8
DEBORAH PRINCE (illustrator from Massachusetts)
Weeping willow study done with technical drawing pen.
This shows the method of repeated or hatched lines to
develop volume and shading.

whole be correct and in proportion. Often
students who concentrate on detail of head
first and then neck and then ear find that
when they get to the legs and tail, they run
off the page. Always work up a gesture
sketch first of the *whole* form, while your
pencil line is still light and while you can
still change your shapes (or still throw
away). Then, when fully satisfied that all is
set, go on and refine lines and form, *still*
working all parts of the drawing to build
them up together. (Refer to the chart in Figure 2.9.)

6. *See negative spaces and forms.* This will
help you with proportions. Check angles
such as neck to shoulder, leg to belly, leaf
stem to branch, and branch to tree trunk.
As described in Figure 2.8, negative space is
the white area (with its own shape) lying
beside all images. In Oriental drawings and
paintings great care is taken in the use of
negative space.

7. *Use foreshortening.* The challenge in
drawing is to make what is three-dimensional still *look* three-dimensional when put
on a flat piece of paper. This is why foreshortening so confuses the beginning student. It helps if you learn to see a particular
form as a flat geometric shape, as was done
in order to draw the leaves in Figure 2.7. To
do this, try squinting or putting a hand over
one eye so that depth perception dimin-
ishes. Try cutting that shape out of paper.
This will help you to see what the negative
space is around the shape, as well as the
dimensions of the form itself. As an exercise, I have students hold their hand in the
vertical profile and then hold it in varied
positions imagining how they would draw
each posture. I even suggest that they draw
those positions. Foreshortening results
when an object lies in more than one plane
or when it has any sort of depth. Since we
have no dimension to our drawing surface,
we must *suggest* it by other means, for
example, by contrast in size and shape.

8. *Use shading.* Another method of indica-
ting forshortening, as well as contrasts in
volume, color, and tone, is by the use of
shading. In field sketching, where not a
great deal of detail work is done, shading is
not as extensively developed as it might be
in other methods of drawing. Shading is
generally applied by laying in a variety of
continuous line strokes, as shown in Figures 1.7, 2.4, 2.8, 2.15, or 2.29. Since clarity
is key in natural history drawing, smudging
or random scribbling can confuse details
and even important identification features.
A less graphic, shaded line is more appropriate when doing expressive sketching,

particularly of landscapes in which form definition is less of an issue.

To shade by this *hatch* method, as it is called, position your wrist firmly on the paper and just move the three fingers holding the pen or pencil. Draw lines in either continuous down strokes (which can only be done with a technical pen) or up and down strokes (a looser method that can be done with pencil as well.) Keep your lines shaded because in this method, line is used to fill in an area of tone (as in Figure 6.21), not to define outline. Therefore, individual strokes should not stand out.

9. *Obtain depth, volume, and tone by shading contrasts.* To make something look dimensional on a flat piece of paper, you need to use a system of contrasts. Contrast in *shape* is one, as just discussed in paragraph 7.

Contrast in *shading* is another. Using the chart in Figure 2.9, notice that what is in the foreground should be either darker *or* lighter than what is in the background, in terms of both tone and lighting. What is in the foreground generally is drawn *more* distinctly because it is closer and what is in the background is drawn *less* distinctly because it is farther away. This is also a trick in attaining a foreshortened image, as explained in Figure 2.6.

10. *Draw from photographs.* It will not always be possible to have the subject you wish to draw right in front of you, posing just the way you wish, and displaying all the details you need to study. As discussed in Chapter 1, photographs, and particularly those you take yourself, are important resources to work from. Use care in choos-

Figure 2.9
General order to follow when sketching any subject.

1. OBSERVATION — analyze form from various positions deciding what side is best to sketch

2. SHAPE — Sketch in principal shapes lightly using gesture technique

3. PROPORTION — Slow down lines, carefully checking angles, negative spaces, shape relationships. Do not go on until these are correct

4. VOLUME and TONE — Contrast of tones to give sense of depth and volume

5. COLOR

6. TEXTURE

	COLOR		TONE		DETAIL	LIGHT	
FOREGROUND	light	dark	pale	dark	more distinct	Shadow	Sunlit
BACKGROUND	dark	light	dark	pale	less distinct	Sunlit	Shadow

caused by aerial perspective in landscape drawing

caused by linear persp. in landscape drawing

7. DETAIL — last

ing your photographs. A subject should not be oddly foreshortened, in confusing shadow, or in too unusual a pose. If for some reason you plan to publish a drawing taken from a photograph, be sure that it has been changed substantially or that you obtain permission from and give full credit to the photographer because of today's copyright laws.

Although photographs have their values, I find it unfortunate that all too many wildlife artists today work largely from photographs with little time spent out in the field. Roger Tory Peterson is quoted as saying, "I never copy from them [photographs] . . . Sketches are more suggestive of what the eventual picture might be. With a sketch you can get rid of the clutter of a photograph; the sketch really shows more the essence of the subject. But photos are important memory jogs."*

11. *Sketch from museum study mounts and skinned specimens.* It is a valuable experience to sketch from museum mounts and skinned specimens. This provides the opportunity to look in detail at an animal's features without worrying that it will move. Be aware that these mounts may be old, that the taxidermist may have stuffed the animal into a position that is not strictly accurate, and that the feather or fur alignment is no longer in place. Dust can also affect the sheen of feathers and fur. And glass eyes change the character of the face. Be sure to label these sketches "from a study mount" and note the museum or lab. I have seen beautifully rendered paintings of animals and plants that must have been done solely from mounts or pressed specimens; a trained eye notices a slightly odd posture, expression, fur or feather alignment, or stiff placement of leaves and petals.

12. *Study other artists' styles.* Since wildlife sketching and drawing is not widely

taught, you will soon find that you need to search out the works of other wildlife artists. Unfortunately, you'll find most examples as illustrations in books and magazines or occasionally on exhibition in art or science museums. Wildlife art, in general, has a way to go before it will be accepted in the mainstream of art. Traditionally, it has been considered more as illustration than as art. Today, the debate still goes on.

It is alright to copy works by other artists, and I have my students do this as part of their regular course of study, *as long as you record below the drawing from whom it was copied.* Browse in the nature or natural science sections of libraries, bookstores, and museum shops. Be sure to look in the children's sections, as many of the good wildlife illustrations appear in stories for the young. Look also in card shops, since many artists are finding cards to be a good outlet for selling and exhibiting their works. And wildlife art is sometimes featured in nature and environmental magazines, as well as in many hunting and sporting journals. (Historically, the sportsperson and hunter have often been the patrons of the wildlife artist.)

It still holds true that those artists who use the field sketching methods described in this book are found predominantly in Europe, particularly in Great Britain, Sweden, and Germany. In these countries, there has long been an interest in nature study and in natural history illustration. As yet, the interest is not comparable in this country. Go into a bookstore today and see the number of illustrated sketchbooks or nature diaries that are coming in from abroad. (Edith Holden's *The Country Diary of an Edwardian Lady*, Keith Brockie's *Wildlife Sketchbook*, or Charles Tunnicliffe's *A Sketchbook of Birds* are just a few titles.) A number of these books were done during the Victorian and Edwardian eras when there seemed to be certain popular interest in recounting one's experiences while roaming the local fields and woodlands.

---

* Patricia Van Gelder, *Wildlife Artists at Work* (New York: Watson-Guptill Publications, 1982), p. 134.

SUGGESTIONS FOR SKETCHING SPECIFIC SUBJECTS

The remaining illustrations in this chapter and their respective captions have been selected as examples of exercises and explanations of ways to sketch inanimate objects, birds and other animals, plants, trees, landscapes, rocks, and sky. Refer back to these illustrations as you read through the rest of the text or as you come upon these subjects when out sketching in various habitats. Instead of including specific exercises for you to do, I prefer that you devise your own, for then you can determine what manner of sketching best suits you.

Study natural history as you study sketching methods. Since field sketching has as its purpose the study of plants and animals and the natural landscape, it is important that you accompany your study of drawing technique with your study of natural history. Many of the illustrators I have mentioned started looking at and drawing nature when they were very young. Nature study has long been a respected part of the British and European school systems. When I was in Scotland studying with John Busby, every artist I met casually said that he or she had been painting birds, plants, or animals since the age of five, six, or seven.

Figure 2.10
Demonstration to students of suggestions for drawing an animal when time allows for a more developed drawing. It is important to know not only animal anatomy and feature details, but also how an animal moves and something of its character. Try as much as possible to draw those animals you have watched alive and in their own environment. Read about their life histories and check a field guide book to make sure of physical details. Approach the study of animals with an intelligence that goes beyond merely wishing to draw accomplished portraits.

Figure 2.11
WILLIAM D. BERRY (Twentieth century Alaskan wildlife artist)
Caribou studies.
Reproduced courtesy of Mark Berry of Berry Studios, Fairbanks.

By relatively simple drawing techniques, Berry has recorded an assemblage of
behavioral postures. Notice the running commentary and parenthetical
statements, "memory," "life and memory." Observe that most of the comments
are about what was happening. In addition to being a wildlife artist, Berry was
a prominent animal behaviorist. Compare his style with Ennion's in Figure
2.15. Both were as much naturalists as they were artists.

Figure 2.12
Studies of several species of birds created to show students how the basic form of all birds derives from a simple egg shape. In the initial sketch you can see that if you draw this shape and tilt it along the proper axis, you will manage a basic posture for a bird. Be sure to set the egg in relation to the branch or whatever the bird is situated on. These were sketched from a field guide, and they demonstrate how book illustrations can help you get the idea of an animals features before drawing it in the field.

Figure 2.13
It is most helpful when studying any animal, to have the opportunity to draw from a skeleton and see how parts fit together underneath fur and flesh. A visit to a natural history museum or to a biology department is highly recommended; for there you will see many species of animal on display.

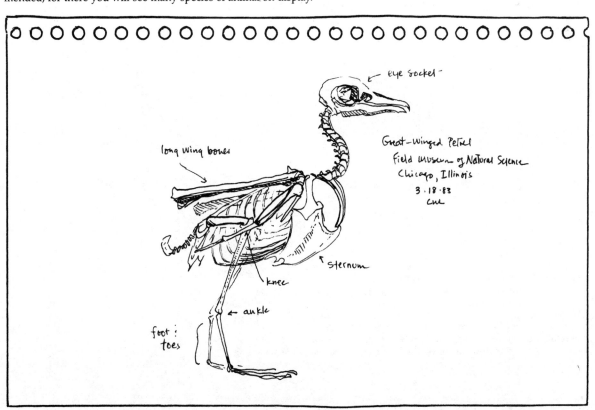

Figure 2.14
Sketches of a starling held in a student's hand.
It is most worthwhile to sketch a bird that is alive and responsive in close
range. This can be done at a zoo, pet store, duck pond, or bird-banding station.
The bird here had been trapped for a school demonstration with sixth-graders.
A student brought it to a drawing class and held it while we sketched. My
notes are intended as aids for students in the techniques of drawing. Students
were asked to write down notes on the information learned while sketching.

Figure 2.15

ERIC ENNION (Twentieth century British artist)
Sketches of puffins reproduced from *The Living birds of Eric Ennion* with commentary by John Busby (London: Victor Gallancz, 1982), p. 124.

Permission to reproduce granted by the family of Eric Ennion.

Beside the sketches Ennion wrote, "Draw as fast and as much as you can while your bird stays put—don't bother about scale. Just draw them as big as they look! And don't rub out, start a new drawing beside the old one."

Busby comments in the text below, "Puffins drawn at sea— by no means easy if you stop to think first! I have vivid memories of tours of the Farnes with Eric drawing like mad while everyone else struggled with cameras. I wonder who saw the most?"

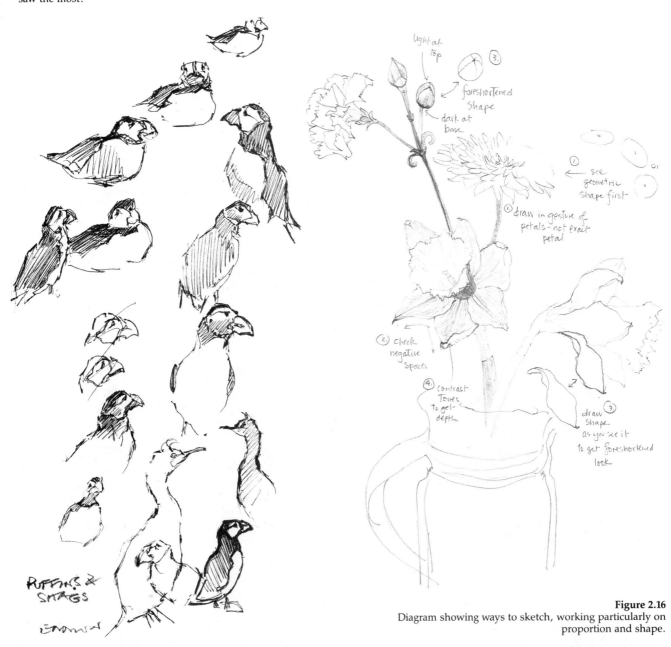

Figure 2.16
Diagram showing ways to sketch, working particularly on proportion and shape.

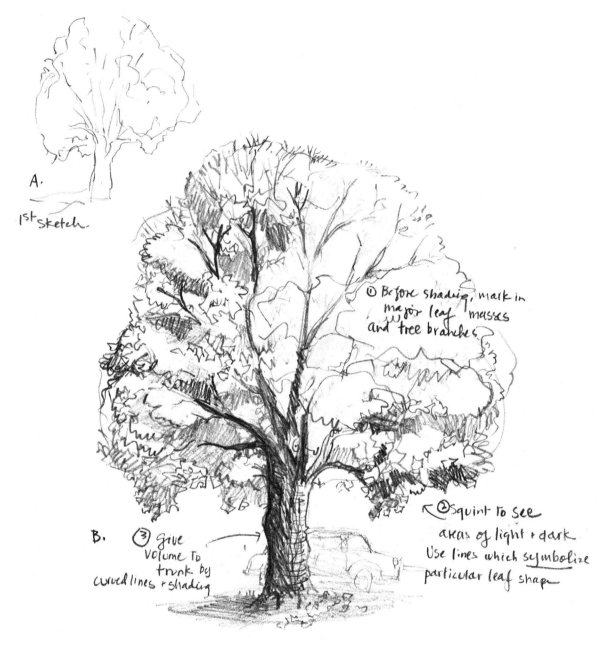

A.

1st sketch.

B. ③ Give
volume to
trunk by
curved lines + shading

① Before shading, mark in
major leaf masses
and tree branches

② squint to see
areas of light + dark
Use lines which symbolize
particular leaf shape

Figure 2.17
Field study of a Norway maple tree in October. The tree is located in the
parking lot of an urban shopping center.

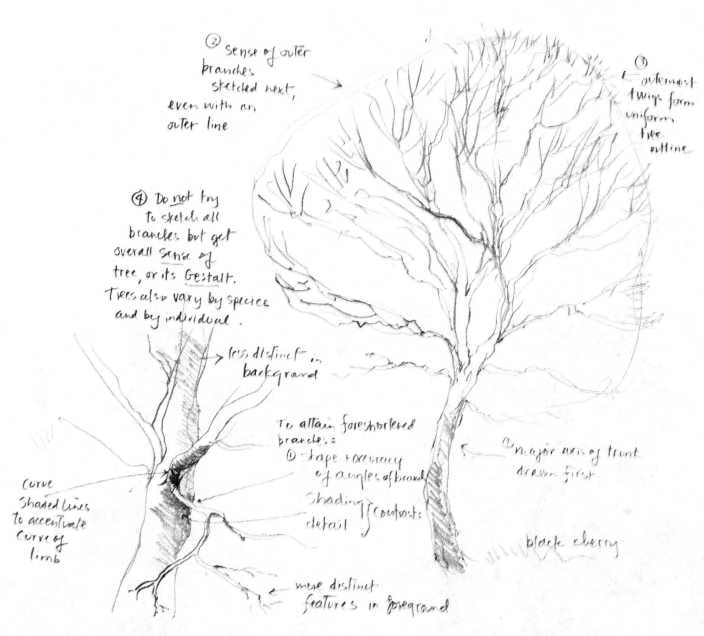

② sense of outer branches sketched next, even with an outer line

③ ← outermost twigs form uniform tree outline

④ Do not try to sketch all branches but get overall sense of tree, or its Gestalt. Trees also vary by species and by individual.

→ less distinct in background

To attain foreshortened branches: =
① shape + accuracy of angles of branch
shading } contrasts
detail

① major axis of trunk drawn first

Curve Shaded lines to accentuate Curve of limb

black cherry

← more distinct features in foreground

Figure 2.18
Class demonstration showing how to draw a winter tree. During a workshop held at Manomet bird observatory, Manomet Massachusetts, participants were interested in using drawing for their field observation work.

Figure 2.19
Experiment with various lines on a scrap of paper to learn ways of symbolizing types of landscape vegetation. Whenever looking at a landscape drawing by another artist, take special note of the symbols and marks they use. Good examples are the drawings by Van Gogh, Rembrandt, Wyeth, Turner, Van Ruisdael, and Lorrain.

Figure 2.20
DEBORAH PRINCE (Illustrator from Massachusetts)
Field study of a white pine (3B Pencil).
The artist intended to achieve a quick gestural impression that specifically says "white pine," and not "hemlock," "red pine," or any other tree. Notice how simply, yet clearly, she has achieved this. (b) The finished drawing taken from Prince's field sketch and drawn with a technical drawing pen.

Figure 2.21
RICHARD GAYTON (Illustrator from California)
Sketch of a California live oak on Canada College Campus,
February 10, 1981 (technical pen).
Answering the question of whether he considered this to be more a drawing
than a sketch, Gayton replied, "The tree sketch is perhaps more rightly a
'study,' although my more formal drawings are usually larger and more
composed. In my own mind it remains a sketch, an informal homage to a
grand and ancient tree." [Personal communication, January 16, 1983.] Note how
the artist has symbolized the leaves on the tree, the texture of the bark, as well
as the various features in the surrounding landscape.

Eric Ennion commented that until he was ten, he avidly copied birds from guide books or drew them from imagination. But from then on "birds, butterflies and moths filled holidays and every minute I could rest from term-time . . . although how much time I spent sketching, how much just watching birds, I could not say. I know I usually slipped a sketchbook into my pocket whenever I went out. . . . Contented and absorbed I roamed the fields and fens round my own home; . . . and where better could a boy evolve his own particular ways of sketching the birds he loved in action?"*

* John Busby, *The Living Birds of Eric Ennion* (London: Victor Gollancz, 1982), p. 113.

Study basic behavior patterns of birds and animals. All birds and animals go through daily routines, just as you do. They also go through seasonal routines, whether they migrate away from your area or just become less evident. Observe their basic patterns: feeding and foraging, resting and sleeping, traveling (seasonal and daily), interacting socially (offensive and defensive), establishing territories, interacting as families (courtship, home maintenance, rearing of young). Learn to recognize what an animal is doing and draw it in that posture (even if you see only a partial view from a nest hole or with its back to you) and not solely in the portrait profile. I have seen so many technically proficient paintings of animals and plants that say absolutely nothing *about* the subject. Keep this in mind next time you go out to draw something. Do not come home without having learned something new. Nature is never boring. It is the uneducated eye that may find it so.

CATEGORIES OF SUBJECTS TO SKETCH
- *Inanimate objects.* See Figures 2.3, 2.6, 4.15, and 7.15.
- *Animals.* See Figures 1.1, 1.12, 2.10, 2.11, 3.5, 4.18, 4.22, 5.15, and 6.9.
- *Birds.* See Figures 2.12, 2.13, 2.14, 2.15, 4.2, 4.4, 5.17, 5.18, 6.26, 7.16, 7.17, 7.18, 7.24, 7.26, and 7.27.
- *Plants.* See Figures 2.7, 2.16, 3.3, 4.8, 5.3, 5.4, 6.6, 6.18, and 7.22.
- *Trees.* See Figures 2.8, 2.17, 2.18, 2.19, 2.20A and B, 2.21, 3.13, 5.6, and 5.12.

LANDSCAPE SUGGESTIONS

Landscapes are perhaps the most difficult subjects in nature to represent, since they involve knowing a fair amount about various artistic principles. To draw trees in the distance, you need to know about perspective and shading. To draw a woodland scene, you need to know something about composition. To draw moving water, you need to know about light and shadow. To draw foliage and grasses, you need a whole repertoire of symbols to suggest a variety of forms. And to draw mountains and rocks, you need to know about mass and volume.

John Carlson says, "We must have design in a picture at the expense of truth. The artist must look to nature for his inspiration, but must rearrange elemental truths into an orderly sequence or progression of interests."* Be less the scientist and more the artist when sketching landscapes. Take liberties and experiment with both techniques and media. No matter how hard you try, you will not be able to replicate that landscape. What is much more interesting is to *interpret* it and to convey your attraction to it, whether it be to its shapes, its varying textures, its colors, or its light and shadows. If, in fact, you do need to document what is there for more scientific purposes, add notes along the margins. Read the suggestions listed below and in Figures 2.24A, B, C, and D. Study the landscapes illustrated throughout this book and, for further books on landscape drawing, refer to the Bibliography.*

In sketching landscapes, keep these things in mind:

1. *Take time to look for a composition* that will be interesting and that has a focus. Squint one eye and hold your hands up, thus providing a frame for your composition, as described in Figure 2.22. Looking through a camera lens can also be helpful. Hold the frame first horizontally and then vertically to see which shape you prefer. Then, sketch out a rough composition, as in Figure 2.24C. Don't just do the first landscape you see. Get up and move around, taking some time to select a scene that not only looks nice but that would make an interesting picture on your paper. The student's sketches in Figure 2.26 were done in her backyard and took all of one hour to do.

* John Carlson, *Carlson's Guide to Landscape Painting* (New York: Dover Publications, 1958), p. 98.

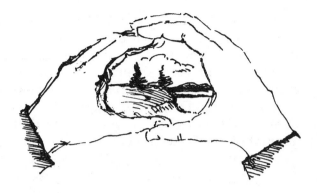

Figure 2.22
By framing a landscape with your fingers, you can
determine the borders of a composition and isolate key
elements and shapes within its format.

2. *Keep your first landscape sketches small.*
Do not make them more than 2″ × 4″ or
3″ × 5″ so as not to have large areas to
cover. I often have students do several one-
minute landscape sketches within pre-
drawn frames, one next to the other, before
going on to a larger and lengthier sketch.
The lengthier sketches should still be no
larger than 6″ × 9″.

3. Keeping in mind the frame of your picture (you can either draw it in first or keep
an area of white paper between your sketch
and the page's edges as Gunnar Brusewtiz
does in Figure 2.27), *begin transferring, with*

Figure 2.23
Landscape studies by a student in her backyard.
Notice how small her frames are (2½″ x 4″), allowing her to work with a
manageable composition that can be filled in rapidly and completed in about
ten minutes. In addition, observe how well the foreground, middleground,
and background have been divided, yet flow into each other.

your mind's eye, the landscape before you into abstract shapes on your paper, as in Figure 2.25.

4. *First, see your composition in terms of these abstract shapes or masses* and separate them into foreground, middleground, background, and sky, as in Figure 2.24B. It is hard for beginning students to make these divisions, but it comes with practice. It helps to squint, for then specific details are blurred and major shapes become more clear. Often, these flat masses, or planes as they are also called, are distinguished by differing tones, light, and shade or in the amount of detail given them.

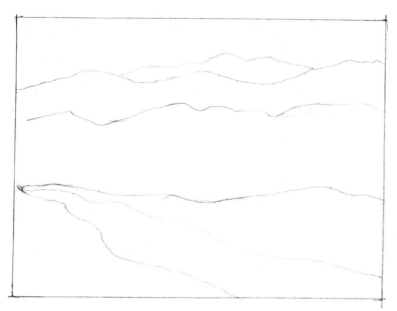

Figure 2.24a
Beneath all good landscapes is a solid composition.

Figure 2.24b
Dividing your landscape into three regions can help establish its compositional structure and can distinguish the contrasts in detail and shading.

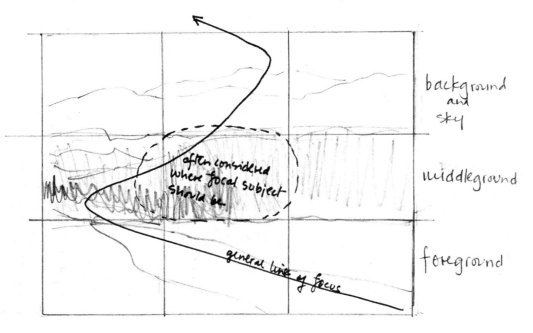

Figure 2.24c
Three-minute gesture sketch, keeping in mind the
formation of the three planes.

Figure 2.24d
A lengthier fifteen-minute sketch done while looking
out the car window on a cold winter day.

29 April 1983
Long Hill,
Beverly, Mass.

Figure 2.25
A student's field study, drawn with a black fine-tipped ball-point pen. First, the student drew the major compositional elements in a postage stamp-sized preliminary sketch. With this for reference, she went on to describe a rather complex subject whch she achieved by eliminating and emphasizing selected subjects that fit within the initial compositional arrangement. We *cannot* replicate nature. We must instead learn the skills for representing. Mention also should be made that with a morning of drawing as the purpose, this particular class had a marvelous opportunity to spend some time in a lush garden habitat that few of them would have visited otherwise.

5. *Generally, what is in the foreground is more distinct and what is in the background is less so* (see Figure 2.9). This has to do with atmospheric perspective. Since a great depth must be attained on the flat surface of your paper, any sort of *contrast* is necessary, whether it be obtained by detail or by lighting. You must essentially trick the eye of the observer into believing there really are miles between the space of just a few inches! *Contrast* is the key word in giving depth to a sketch and is accomplished by a striking variation in definition of detail and in the color range within shapes. The *Hunting Scene* attributed to Gainsborough (Fig-ure 2.26) shows how the artist utilized sharp contrasts of light and shade, detail, and variations between planes to achieve a marked sense of distance. Notice also how your eye moves easily through the picture, aided by carefully placed subjects such as the path, hedgerow, and shaded areas.

6. *Linear perspective exists where objects in the foreground are larger than objects farther away.* Sometimes artists will introduce retreating lines as fences, telephone poles, stone walls, paths, or streams to help emphasize a retreating distance, as in Figures 2.26, 2.27 and 2.28.

Figure 2.26
THOMAS GAINSBOROUGH (eighteenth century British artist)
Hunting Scene (charcoal pencil).
Courtesy of the Museum of Fine Arts, Boston.

It was common practice in Gainsborough's time for artists to carry small sketchbooks with them to jot down an idea for a future painting, when a subject caught their interest. Perhaps this sketch later became a painting or was one of many studies of this region done by Gainsborough.

Figure 2.27
GUNNAR BRUSEWITZ (contemporary Swedish artist/naturalist)
Mariedel, April 14, 1978
This pencil sketch was drawn outdoors and the color wash was added later.
Brusewitz made an interesting point in one of his letters: "Nature art is a never-
ceasing searching for the right expression for an experience, if you understand
what I mean. An 'experience' can be the swift sight of a bird in flight or a deer
disappearing in the twilight. You have to catch it very rapidly, and if you don't
find the right expression for it at once, it can be difficult. Maybe that is the most
fascinating [part] of the whole business." [Personal communication, December
20, 1982]

7. *A landscape sketch in effect tells a story and so should be clear enough to be easily read.* Thus, set your shapes of foreground, middleground, and background so that they connect with one another. Keeping details away from the outer edges, focus the eye's attention more in the center of the picture.

8. *Deciding what to put in is as important as what to leave out.* As Vernon Blake says,

> "The first error that most beginners make is to deliberately sit down in front of an object of their admiration and draw it all. . . . Now all sketching is more or less impressionistic in nature; it aims more at

suggestion of things than at categoric representation of them; for the latter, as a rule, the sketcher has not time enough."[3]

9. *After setting up your major composition shapes and before putting in details, mark in the various tones* determined by atmospheric perspective, the presence of light and shadow, as well as the overall harmonies of your composition. (It is all right to rearrange these tonalities and also various features in a landscape to make a more unified

[3] Vernon Blake, *The Way to Sketch* (New York: Dover Publications, 1981), p. 33.

composition as long as the major elements are accurately represented.)

10. *Keep major details in the foreground* with receding emphasis as you go toward the background. This clarity of image is affected by *atmospheric perspective*, as it is called in artistic terminology.

11. *Experiment with varieties of marks to suggest grasses, trees, leaves, and so forth.* You cannot possibly draw all that you see and so you must quickly learn convincing ways of symbolizing. Look at the strokes used in Figures 2.4 and 2.28 and even copy them to get their shapes into your hand. A master of the symbol was Vincent Van Gogh, as evidenced in his small pen and ink landscape sketches.

12. *Do not spend more than half an hour on a landscape study.* The intention is to keep the impression fresh and spontaneous. It will begin to look overworked if you go much longer. When in doubt, leave it and return

Figure 2.28

EARL THOLLANDER

Adamsville, Rhode Island (ink wash) from the book, *Back Roads of New England* by the artist (New York: Clarkson N. Potter, Inc., 1982).

Used by permission of Clarkson N. Potter, Inc.

Often, inspiration for new ways to sketch and draw can be found by browsing in bookstores or libraries. A wide range of illustation techniques appears in print today. Be open to trying different methods. Note how the artist has symbolized vegetation forms, just suggesting the shapes of trees. Sometimes it's worthwhile to buy a book, not merely for the text, but also to learn from the illustrations.

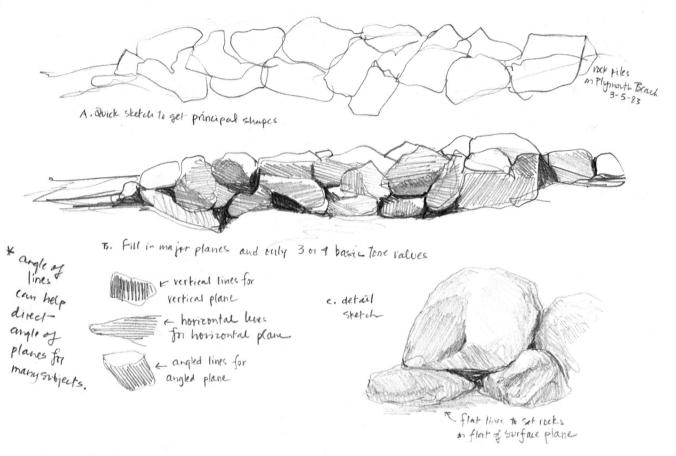

A. Quick sketch to get principal shapes

rock piles
on Plymouth Beach
3-5-83

B. Fill in major planes and only 3 or 4 basic tone values

* angle of lines can help direct—angle of planes for many subjects.

← vertical lines for vertical plane

← horizontal lines for horizontal plane

← angled lines for angled plane

c. detail sketch

↖ flat lines to set rocks on flat of surface plane

Figure 2.29
Ways to draw rocks and to shade the angles of the surface planes. When drawing rocks, it is important to locate the source of light and see how it sends shadow patterns across the forms. It is equally important to understand that these rocks have mass and volume. Sometimes, therefore, it is necessary to rearrange the existing light patterns in order to describe a convincing picture of rock mass on your paper. To do this, think of rocks as cubes with a top, bottom, and sides. Each of these surfaces must be treated with a different tone to establish their contrasts. (Refer also to Figures 6.16a, 6.20, and 6.21.)

later, perhaps once back home, while the memory is still fresh and you have more time to consider drawing technique. You can always add to a drawing but it often ruins one when you start erasing and fussing. If you do not like the initial sketch, do another one. (So often the best teacher is the *next* drawing.)

13. *Try combining several media* such as a felt-tipped pen for line work and pencil for tonal color (as was done in Figure 7.15). Also, pencil and colored pencil or pencil with simple washes (as in Figure 2.27) can be effective if you want to add a bit of color.

14. *Some students find it helpful, when learning to draw landscapes, to spend time copying from photographs.* There, a composition has already been chosen, and often the various planes are more easily distinguishable. Both black and white and color are useful. A good way to learn tree silhouettes is to take tracing paper and copy over the outlines of a winter tree from a clear black and white photograph.

15. *Study the rocks* done in Figure 2.29 and in Figures 6.16A, 6.20, 6.21, and 7.4.

16. *Weather conditions landscapes in both scientific and artistic terms.* In winter, a scene may bear little resemblance to its summer look. Similarly, a cloudy day or a sunny day can totally change the mood of a place. That is why getting to know one small habitat can be so interesting—it is never the same from day to day. When you draw a landscape, take note of the weather as well as the time of day. Be aware of whether it is windy or about to storm. Locate the direction of the sun and see what shadows it is casting. Whenever appropriate, draw in the sky and its cloud formations. A landscape can change dramatically, whether it be a dark and stormy sky or a bright and cloudless sky.

Clouds are drawn mostly by building up the shaded areas within their mass and in the surrounding sky. Use the side of the pencil and make a series of soft, rolling lines. Look at the clouds in Figures 2.30A and B, 6.19, 6.20, 7.8, and 7.11.

17. *Look at the study sketches of the great land-*

Figure 2.30a
Diagram of cloud formations.

Figure 2.30b
Large cumulus and cumulonimbus clouds gather over open expanses of land. When drawing clouds, keep in mind the land formations, weather conditions, location of the sun, and time of day. Clouds should be sketched with close attention to lights and darks, and with an impression of airy massiveness. Often a landscape is given greater depth by adding clouds to the sky or by setting clouds so that they connect behind a ridge or land mass. (Refer also to Figures 6.19, 6.20, 7.8, 7.9, and 7.11.)

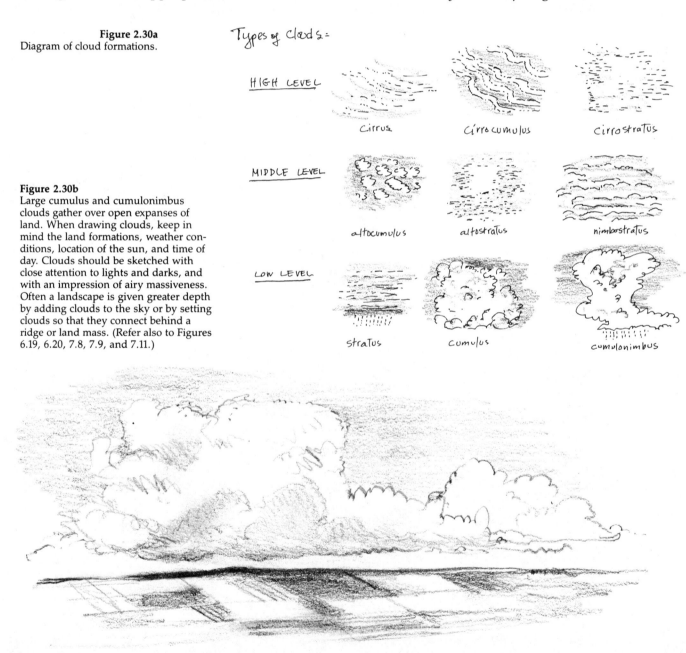

scape painters such as Rembrandt (Dutch), J.M.W. Turner (British), Constable (British), Corot (French), Van Gogh (Dutch), Winslow Homer (American), Wyeth (American). Do not overlook the landscape painters of the Far East with their distinctly nonwestern attitudes toward nature. And pay special attention to the group of American landscape painters called the Hudson River school, active during the nineteenth century. Artists like Cole, Bierstadt, Church, Durand, and Cropsey broke with the tradition of painting landscapes only from indoors and went outside with their sketchbooks to be inspired by nature directly.

Those of you who think that the art of field sketching is a new method should go to the sketchbooks of these masters and see what a wealthy tradition it has. It is, in fact, a real misfortune that so many artists today have lost this inheritance and no longer care to study nature so directly.

Figure 2.31
EDWARD B. STEWART (nineteenth century American painter)
Landscape sketch done in France, August 1886.
Permission to reproduce given by Elizabeth S. Ellis.

This sketch was drawn with a very soft pencil in a 4½" x 7½" sketchbook. Close attention should be paid to the marvelous color and mood contained in this small study, where tone rather than outline was used to define images. Compare Stewart's style with one of his contemporaries, William H. Walker, and see the richness of pencil tone employed by both artists.

Chapter 3
Keeping a Field Journal

A field journal differs from a field sketchbook in that it is used as an ongoing record of observations from a specific place and throughout either a calendar year or a particular period of time. Whereas a journal is kept in sequence, a sketchbook may not be because notations of date, location, time, and weather are carefully documented. I have used my journals to learn about natural history on a daily basis and often do not consider my entries to be drawings at all. In fact, my style can be quite childlike in attempt (conscious or otherwise) to break away from my own pressure to create "a good drawing."

As in the sketchbook, journal entries can be quick jottings or lengthy studies. They can be done indoors as well as outdoors. They can be done by the biology student and the art student alike. The major point to keep in mind is that when doing this form of study, you are making nature your subject of learning and using drawing

as the process. If it helps, keep a separate drawing pad for your studies of nature that are less season- and location-based and represent more your interest in learning the techniques for drawing in addition to sketching.

Most of what I have learned about nature and its processes has come from the experiences I have had using my journals. For four years on a monthly basis, I illustrated a page for the Massachusetts Audubon Society's newsletter, *Sanctuary*, entitled "Notes from a Field Sketchbook" (see Figure 4.1B). Most of these observations derived from entries I had made in my journals. As an artist, I learn best about the natural world by drawing it. Since there is a lot of written information that is interesting to record, by combining writing and drawing, a good amount of knowledge can be stored. In a phone conversation in which we discussed my desire to reproduce some of his work in this book, Robert Bateman, the Canadian wildlife artist, told me, "I would send you one of my paintings, valued at thousands of dollars, before I would send you my original field sketches." In Chapter 8 are reproduced examples of his sketchbook pages.

Although I use an assemblage of sketchbooks for a variety of purposes, I use a journal when documenting the seasonal observations of the two places where we live, rural Vermont and urban Cambridge. (These were published in 1981 as *Notes from a Naturalist's Sketchbook*.) Within the last few years, partially because of the popularity of Edith Holden's *The Country Diary of an Edwardian Lady*, there has been a growing interest in published nature diaries. You should have no difficulty either in a

Figure 3.1
Take advantage of moments like these to record in your journal. Although I watched for no more than ten minutes, I saw a surprising amount of activity. By noting it in my journal, I could document what I had seen, so that if any additional bird activity occurred, I could build a sequence of accumulated information. When looking back in journals of past years, it is interesting to see on which days similar behaviors were observed.

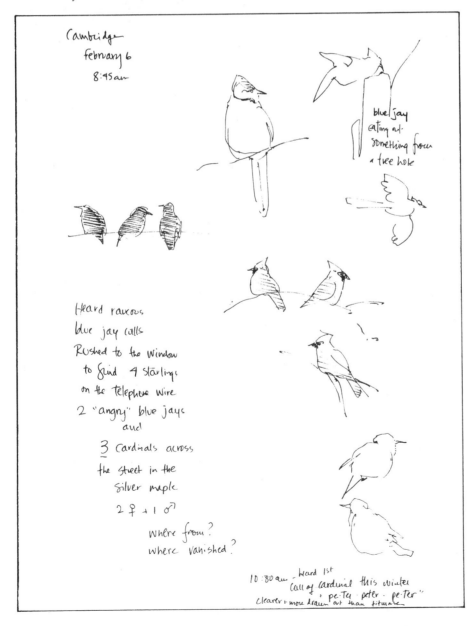

bookstore or library finding sources for inspiration in setting up your own journal. Of course, there are many fine written journals by numerous nature writers that can be read in conjunction with your studies. (See the Bibliography for several names and titles.)

Keeping journals helps us consider the seasons in terms of cycles and not simply as disconnected events. It is exciting to begin a new journal, full of empty pages, and wonder what the year's observations will bring when the book is completed. Likewise, it is fascinating to go through past journals, and, despite apparent changes in the years, discover that the crocuses reappeared on around the same date and, similarly, wood frogs began their spring croaking, geese flew south on fall migration, and goldenrod once again appeared year upon year within a few days' time.

If I have missed a few weeks, I feel the need to catch up on what has happened around me during that time. I keep the year's journal right on my desk, whereas my various drawing pads lie in disarray all over the study. In just a few minutes I can recount the essential events without feeling I must produce much of anything in the way of a drawing. I have been known to add entries while in the midst of something else if there is an interesting event to watch for a moment.

I have pinned over my desk a quotation of Oliver Wendell Holmes's that I reread often: ''Those who are really awake to the sights and sounds which the progression of the months offers them find endless entertainment and instruction.''

SETTING UP A FIELD JOURNAL

1. Drawing equipment should include what is described in Chapter 1 and illustrated in Figure 1.2. Although it is preferable to use a hardbound book because of its durability and booklike characteristics, some students still prefer to use spiral sketchbooks. While I recommend the 8½″ × 11″ size for either, the 6″ × 9″ or the 11″ × 14″ sizes can be used. Some students find that until they have enough confidence to begin a more permanent record, they prefer to do their sketches on loose 8″ × 11″ sheets that they keep together and at some point tape into a bound book. I recommend that you do not, at first, get too concerned over the caliber of your drawings but just jump in. It is the *whole* journal you will be looking at and not just a few individual pages. People should judge the information contained within and not the drawing ability!

2. Leave the first page blank. Then, set up the second page as a title page, entering the date begun, location, your name, and anything about the journal's intent you might wish to note. One of my books has as its title page this statement: ''Book #3. Another cycle of the seasons has begun. These pages are waiting to watch the unfoldings of the coming year. Winter, spring, summer, fall will flow through this book with the affirmation that life goes on, always fascinating, never without event or challenge. [Granville, Vermont, January 13, 1979].''

3. I recommend consistently setting up your pages with date, location, time, weather, approximate temperature, and any other appropriate comments at the top left or right of the paper. A uniformity is established and the calendar can be easily read that way. (See Figures 3.18 and 5.1. Figure 3.13 was done by artists after reading my *Notes from a Naturalist's Sketchbook*.)

4. Do not crowd the page with too many sketches or leave it looking sparse. Determine your own balance between writing and drawing, making sure not to have too much writing, or it will no longer be a sketch journal.

5. Draw with whatever tool is most handy. If something is happening that is worth observing, use what lies nearest, be

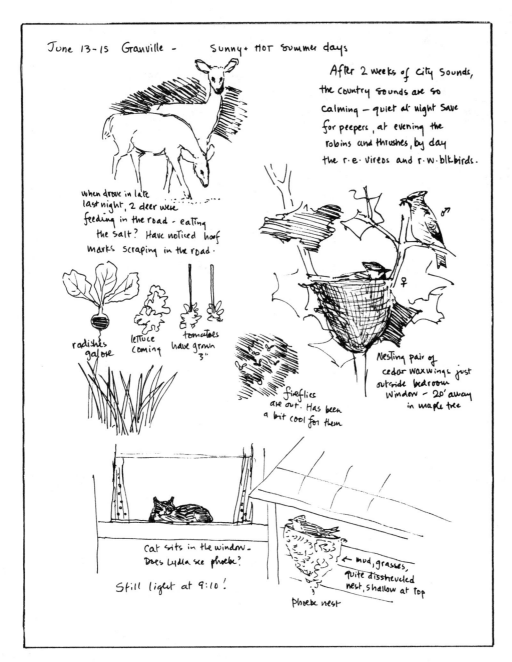

Figure 3.2
This page was entered at the end of a busy weekend when there had been no time to draw. Notes were put down quickly, as recordings from memory of just the key elements characterizing a weekend's events outdoors.

it a child's crayon or the back of an envelope. You can copy it over or tape it into your journal later. (See Figure 5.5.)

6. Be as accurate as you can in recording the identifiable features such as shape of a leaf, markings on a bird, or where an animal is and what it is doing. Even if the drawing is crude, the description of the postures is crucial in the investigation of what was going on.

7. Keep your journal nearby and try to do an entry a day, or at least once a week.

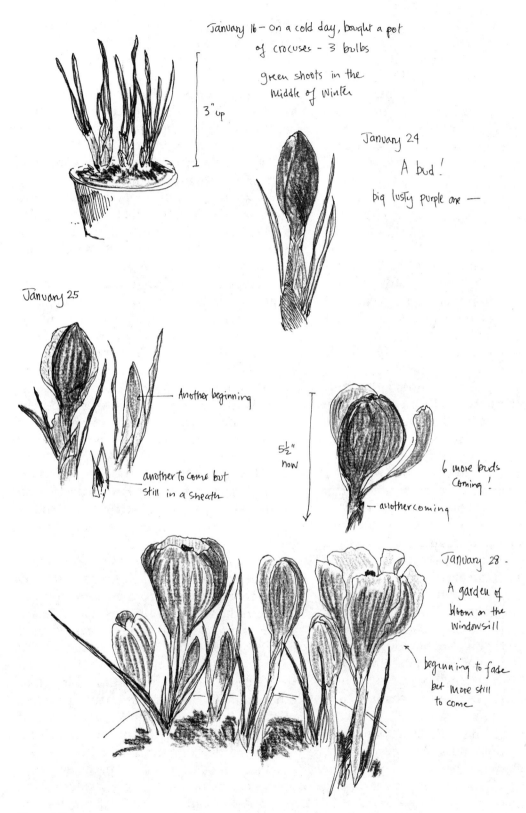

January 16 — on a cold day, bought a pot
of crocuses - 3 bulbs

green shoots in the
middle of winter

3" up

January 24

A bud!

big lusty purple one —

January 25

Another beginning

another to come but
still in a sheath

5½"
now

6 more buds
coming!

another coming

January 28 -

A garden of
bloom on the
windowsill

beginning to fade
but more still
to come

Figure 3.3
Blooming plants can be observed in a sequence indoors and at any time of the
year. This sketch was done with technical pen and colored pencil.

Even if it is only a brief sketch, such as in Figure 3.1, it is enough to get you engaged for a moment with the world outdoors. As professed in the philosophy of meditation, twenty minutes of such contemplation can smooth out the wrinkles from numerous hours of stress. Often I use drawing to bring quiet to my day and to take some time for reflection on a nonhuman subject.

SUBJECTS TO STUDY

1. Keep a journal as your textbook for studying nature, its shifts and changes throughout a complete season or year. Use the journal to sharpen your perceptions and your questioning eye. Do not pass through a day without noticing at least one event of nature, whether it be an ant crawling along a sidewalk or a bird singing on a wire. No matter how small or large the incident, there is a life involved and a purpose to the activity. Where has the ant come from and does it come from a colony? Why is the bird singing and does it have a mate? Do not feel you have to be a biologist or have to know a certain amount already to begin making your own simple observations of what is happening, and happening continually, right in your immediate environment. (I amazed myself the first time I tried to draw an ant and discovered I had not the *slightest* idea about its anatomy. In all insects, I soon found, the legs all come out of just the thorax. My first one had legs attached to both thorax and abdomen. It is fascinating how quickly you discover how little you have observed once you start drawing something.)

A friend, Donald Stokes, wanted to learn about nature and so he wrote a book entitled *A Guide to Nature in Winter*. He chose winter because, of all the seasons, it is the least complex to observe for the beginner, and he chose his native New England as the location. I began keeping sketchbook journals, by his inspiration, because I, too, wanted to learn about nature and had been looking for a vehicle that would help focus my study. Together we formed a Naturalists' Group that met monthly to share observations and to learn together more about the natural history of our region. From those meetings came the most interesting assortment of bits and pieces about butterflies, pollination, gene selection, bird migration, ice crystals, beaver dams, and so forth. If you are going to begin a study of nature it can be most helpful to do it with a few others.

2. Keep a journal of a particular place where you walk frequently so that you have the opportunity to study the subtle shifts of seasonal and weather changes. This place could be around your neighborhood, in a particular park, or in your own backyard.

3. If you are housebound or an invalid, journals can be wonderful projects to help get you away from your concerns and to help focus you for a while on the larger processes occurring outdoors. A woman who was bedridden after a serious operation wrote to me to say that her recovery was made easier by being able to watch the daily activities of the squirrels and blue jays in the oaks outside her window.

A student of mine documented her hospital stay with small sketches of objects in the room, flowers from visitors, and the view out the window. Bird feeders, if set up just outside a bedside window, can provide hours of observing activities during the winter. A backyard that has been planted with trees and flowers to attract birds and other animals can be a naturalist's paradise of things to observe and to document. If you are confined to the house for several seasons, a daily or even weekly check on what's going on outside a particular window can provide a great deal of information about the natural world at large for the housebound artist/naturalist.

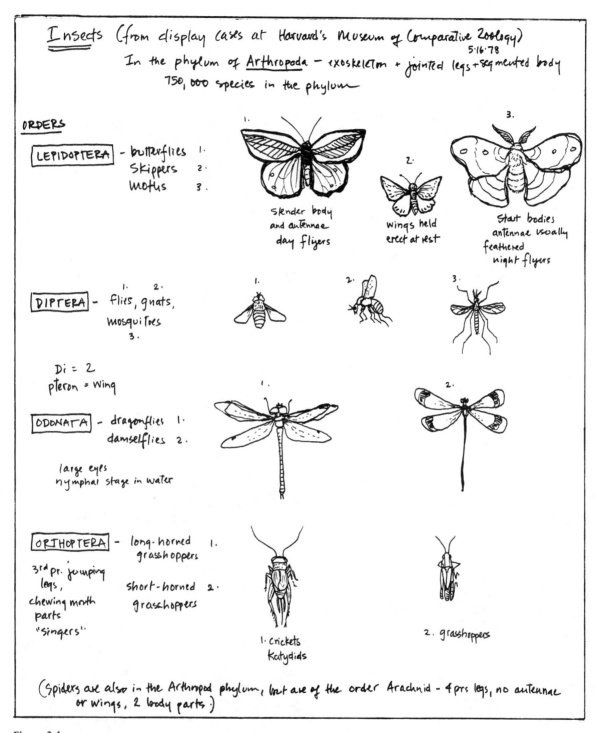

Insects (from display cases at Harvard's Museum of Comparative Zoology)
5·16·78
In the phylum of <u>Arthropoda</u> — exoskeleton + jointed legs + segmented body
750,000 species in the phylum

<u>ORDERS</u>

LEPIDOPTERA — butterflies 1.
Skippers 2.
Moths 3.

1. Slender body
and antennae
day flyers

2. wings held
erect at rest

3. Stout bodies
antennae usually
feathered
night flyers

DIPTERA — flies, gnats,
mosquitoes
1. 2. 3.

Di = 2
pteron = wing

ODONATA — dragonflies 1.
damselflies 2.

large eyes
nymphal stage in water

ORTHOPTERA — long-horned 1.
grasshoppers

3rd pr. jumping
legs,

short-horned 2.
grasshoppers

chewing mouth
parts

"singers"

1. crickets
Katydids

2. grasshoppers

(Spiders are also in the Arthropod phylum, but are of the order Arachnid — 4 prs legs, no antennae
or wings, 2 body parts.)

Figure 3.4
When first learning insect orders, I found that by drawing each shape I could
learn them more effectively.

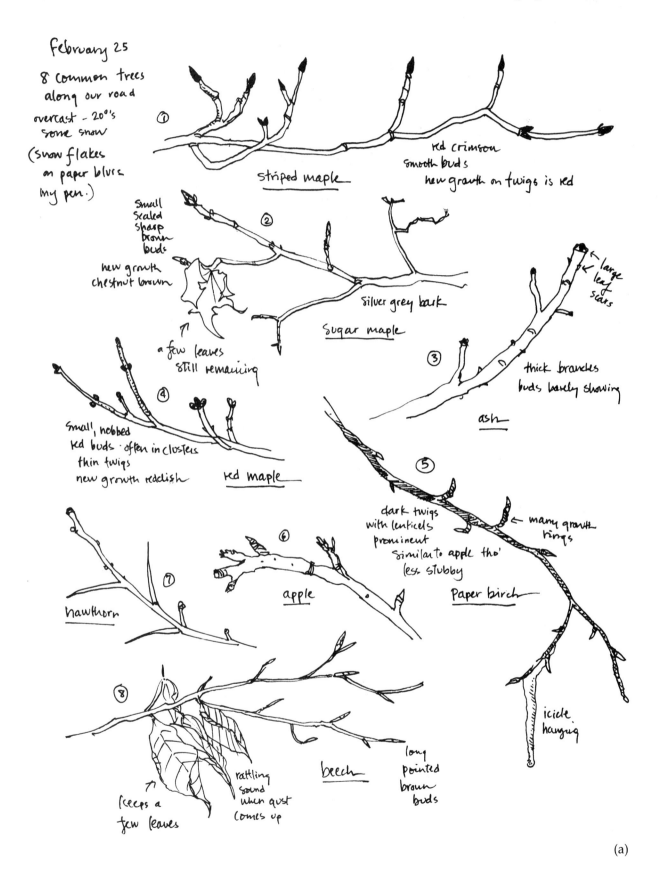

February 25

8 common trees
along our road

overcast - 20°'s
some snow

(snow flakes
on paper blurs
my pen.)

① striped maple
red crimson
smooth buds
new growth on twigs is red

Small scaled sharp brown buds

new growth chestnut brown

② silver grey bark
Sugar maple

a few leaves still remaining

← large leaf scars

③ thick branches
buds barely showing
ash

④ red maple
Small, nobbed red buds · often in clusters
thin twigs
new growth reddish

⑤ dark twigs with lenticels prominent similar to apple tho' less stubby
← many growth rings
Paper birch

icicle hanging

⑥ apple

⑦ hawthorn

⑧ beech
keeps a few leaves
rattling sound when gust comes up
long pointed brown buds

(a)

Figure 3.5
A, B, and C were all drawn while
walking along our road, journal in hand.
It was cold and snowing a bit. I could
only draw a few minutes before having
to blow on my hands and walk quickly to
warm up. Again, sketching is used here
for observation purposes and not for
producing anything to bank
a reputation on!

beaver lodge and dam in snow
2-25-83

(b)

(c)

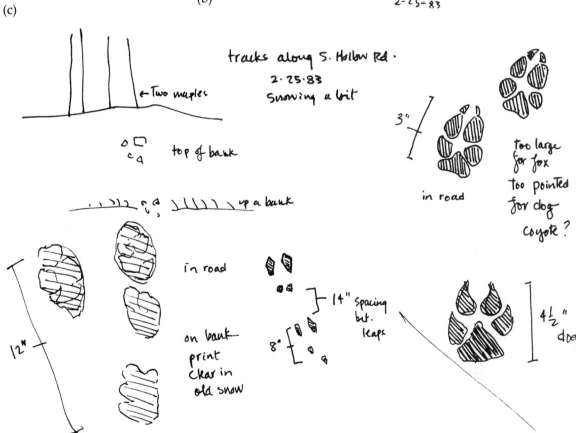

← Two maples

top of bank

up a bank

in road

on bank
print
clear in
old snow

12"

tracks along S. Hollow Rd.
2·25·83
Snowing a bit

3"

in road

too large
for fox
too pointed
for dog
coyote?

14" spacing
bet.
leaps

8"

$4\frac{1}{2}$"
dog

Figure 3.6
ALAN JOHNSTON (English amateur ornithologist)
Sketchbook page from a 4″ x 5¾″ pocket journal.
Johnston's sketchbook contains many small sketches such as
these which carefully document his observations of one
particular nature reserve. This manner of study sketching
can be most useful in scientific field work where daily
accounting is critical. The method of keeping sketchbooks
and nature diaries seems to be more common in England
than in this country. In England nature study is a popular
subject particularly for those who live in the countryside.
Often it is a part of school curriculum.

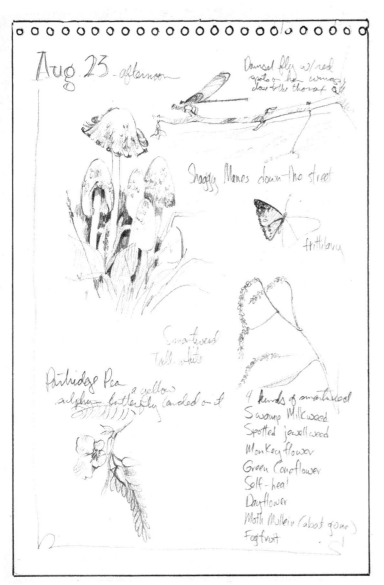

Figure 3.7
CATHY JOHNSON (professional illustrator from Missouri)
A field journal page.
Observe how the artist has made note of the additional
plants found in the area, and has included them in the
overall design of her page.

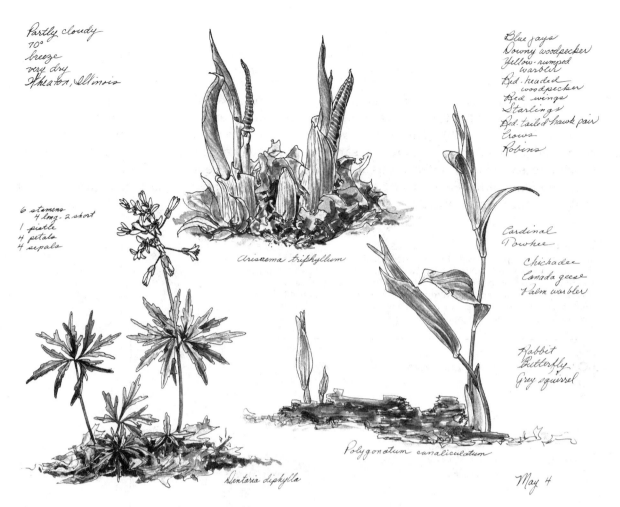

Partly cloudy
70°
breeze
very dry
Wheaton, Illinois

6 stamens
4 long - 2 short
1 pistle
4 petals
4 sepals

Blue jays
Downy woodpecker
Yellow-rumped warbler
Red-headed woodpecker
Red wings
Starlings
Red-tailed hawk pair
Crows
Robins

Cardinal
Towhee
Chickadee
Canada geese
Palm warbler

Rabbit
Butterfly
Grey squirrel

Arisaema triphyllum

Dentaria diphylla

Polygonatum canaliculatum

May 4

Figure 3.8
ROBERTA L. SIMONDS (technical illustrator from Illinois)
Field page drawn with technical pen and watercolor wash.

Figure 3.9
A student of mine keeps a journal of her fresh-water
aquarium. Every few days she makes an entry similar to this
one. If unable to get outdoors, aquariums can be fascinating
micro-habitats to watch. Similar forms of journals can be kept
in a biology classroom, by the entire class or by individual
students.

18
April 17, 1982

Looking at material from Peacock Farm Marsh.
Spirogyra filaments + scrapings from cattail leaf.

This is Testudinella
a Rotifer.

dorsal

about 360 μ

side

Note: Later measurements 180 μ.

flexible. something moves
at the tip. It's cilia.

Ventral

about 180 μ
note claws

A water bear
or Tardigrade!
First one I've found
myself.

very flexible body

membrane

Long tail is flexible as is whole body
cilia beat constantly. Membrane
undulates
Moves fairly slowly - now, at least.
Note longitudinal dotted lines.

A protozoan - didn't get size

Lots of Gastrotrichs here, too. Many protozoa
+ rotifers of the more common type.

4. Keep a journal of a specific habitat during a specific period of time (as was done in Figures 3.10 and 4.20). This could be a river's edge, a freshwater pond, a sandy beach and salt marsh, a deciduous woods, or an open meadow. First, make a list of the most evident plants, animals, and geologic features. Keep records of weather, temperature, and seasonal changes. Sketch subjects that characterize the location, are engaged in some sort of activity, or show signs of some sort of change. See the subjects listed in the chart in Figure 3.16 for things to observe.

Figure 3.10
When I drew this page, I was studying the habitat of a specific area of deciduous woods and old pastureland as it changed from late winter to spring. I went there daily, while my son was still young enough to be carried in a backpack. The sketching seemed to fascinate him, and the chance to be outdoors kept us both happy. I would stay for no longer than one hour, but that was enough to get in a lot of observing time.

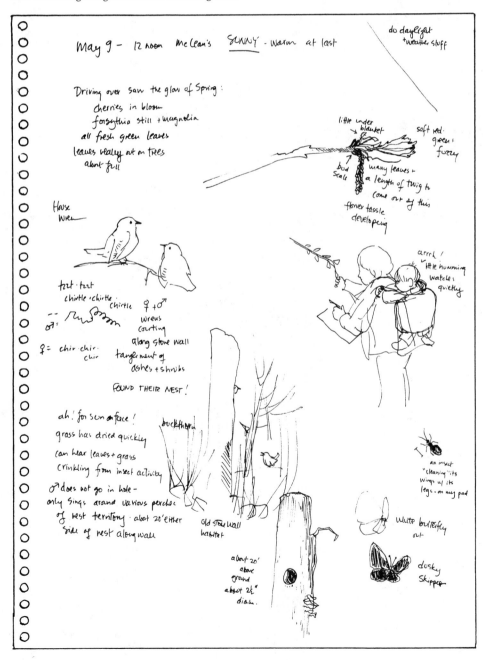

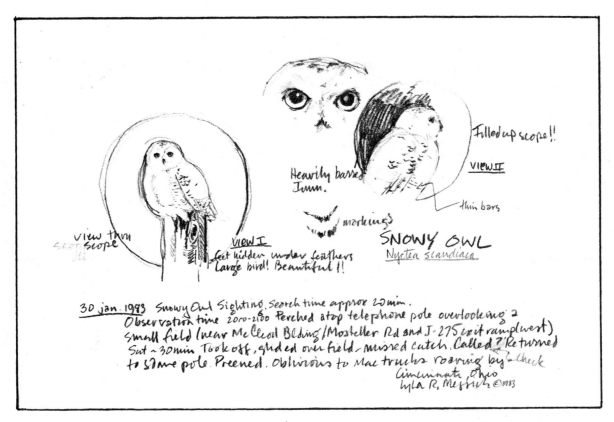

Figure 3.11
One way to record the sighting of a bird is by the method Lyla R. Messick, a biological illustrator from Ohio, used here, working in pencil.

Figure 3.12
Entries in a student's field journal. The March 6 entry was drawn from a hotel window in Killington, Vermont. The next entry was drawn at home in Jackson, New Hampshire. Both sketches were drawn in felt-tipped pen over a preliminary sketch in pencil.

5. Journals can be kept while traveling or on vacation. (See Chapter 6 for how to sketch specific habitats.) Though time may be brief, an experience often is better remembered when drawn rather than photographed. It can also become a focus for a trip. I would love to roam this county and sketch a journal of my travels. Earl Thollander did just that in his illustrated series of travel books, *Back Roads of New England, . . . of Oregon, . . . of Texas, . . . of Washington, . . . of California* (see Figure 2.28).

6. Simple journals can be kept by children or with children. Particularly if traveling, journals can help children learn about

Figure 3.13
STEVE LINDELL (British research chemist)
As he traveled across the United States for the first time, Steve kept a field sketch journal of his observations. A felt-tipped pen and an 8½" x 11" hardbound sketchbook were used.

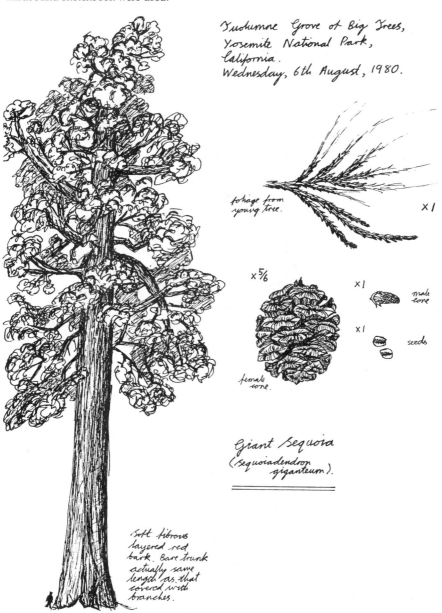

Tuolumne Grove of Big Trees,
Yosemite National Park,
California.
Wednesday, 6th August, 1980.

foliage from young tree.   x1

x⅚

x1 male cone

x1 seeds

female cone.

Giant Sequoia
(sequoiadendron giganteum).

soft fibrous layered red bark. Bare trunk actually same length as that covered with branches.

Figure 3.14
Fourth graders making field journal pages.

where they are going and can give a focus to the trip that has many educational as well as recreational possibilities. When I was ten, our family drove across the country, from Pennsylvania to California and back again. My sisters and I kept written and sketched journals of the entire trip, and to pass the long hours, we did a lot of drawing in the car. To this day, the trip is vivid in my memory and I know it is because each day I put something in my diary.

KEEPING JOURNALS IN THE CLASSROOM OR BIOLOGY LAB

Setting up journals that focus on a study of the environment immediately around the school and throughout the seasons of the school year can provide a means for students to become more aware of the landscape around them and can offer yet another way of combining science, math, English, and even local history. Depending on the age of the class, the time allowed, and the imagination of the teacher, an entire curriculum can be planned around journal study using no more than the school's property. If budgets allow, com-

parison studies can be made by occasional trips to contrasting sites.

If the classroom is a biology lab, field collections and observations can be subjects for continuing studies on a higher level of science. If students are in high school or college, important connections can be made between the studies of natural history (sometimes called field biology, general biology, or even ecology) and the specific subjects of geology, ornithology, botany, or zoology. Robert L. Smith, in his preface to *Ecology and Field Biology*, makes this important point:

> Actually, natural history, field biology, or ecology, call it what you will, should be a part of the education not only of every biologist but also of every chemist, physicist, engineer, lawyer, teacher, agricultural and forestry student, and liberal arts student. It should, in sum, be a part of the liberal education. The reason is simple. As we become more and more engrossed in technology, in our own chrome-plated civilization, we tend to forget that man is a part of nature. . . . In the end, it is the ecological half of biology, rather than molecular biology, that holds the key to the future of man. *

* Robert L. Smith, *Ecology and Field Biology* (New York: Harper & Row, Publishers, 1966), p. viii.

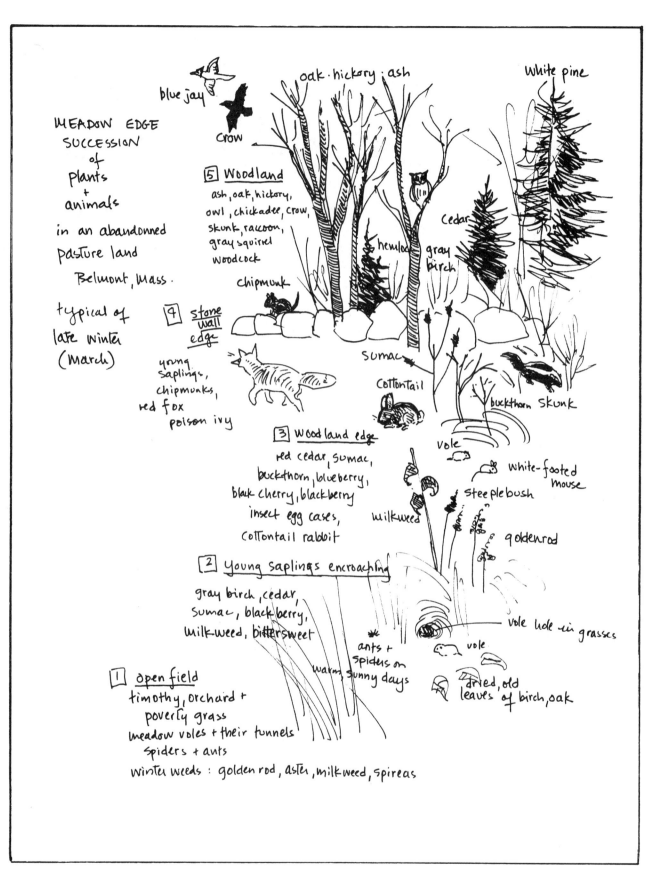

blue jay

crow

oak · hickory · ash

white pine

MEADOW EDGE
SUCCESSION
of
plants
+
animals

in an abandonned
pasture land

Belmont, Mass.

typical of
late winter
(March)

⑤ Woodland
ash, oak, hickory,
owl, chickadee, crow,
skunk, raccoon,
gray squirrel
woodcock

chipmunk

④ stone
wall
edge

young
saplings,
chipmunks,
red fox
poison ivy

cedar

hemlock   gray
birch

sumac

cottontail

buckthorn skunk

vole

③ Woodland edge
red cedar, sumac,
buckthorn, blueberry,
black cherry, blackberry
insect egg cases,
cottontail rabbit

white-footed
mouse

steeplebush

milkweed

goldenrod

② young saplings encroaching

gray birch, cedar,
sumac, blackberry,
milkweed, bittersweet

ants +
spiders on
warm sunny days

vole hole in grasses

vole

① open field
timothy, orchard +
poverty grass
meadow voles + their tunnels
spiders + ants
winter weeds : golden rod, aster, milkweed, spireas

dried, old
leaves of birch, oak

Figure 3.15
Diagrams can be drawn at varying skill levels, describing to students the
features of a specific habitat. Illustrations make a page more interesting to read.

	SUBURBS	MEADOW & PRAIRIE	MOUNTAINS & WOODLAND	CITY
March·April·May SPRING	first buds beginning to swell early flowers to bloom dates of first birds seen returning + nesting first trees to bloom + leaf out signs of animal activity weather changes night sounds + smells	first grasses to reappear sequence of flowers blooming early insects + their activities night activity of animals – woodcock·frogs, raccoon pond or stream life – insects + plants bird activity	altitudes at which snow retreats first flowers to bloom – how altitude and sunlight affects this returning birds + nesting activity insect activity sounds & smells evidence of animal activity evidence of effects of winter	length of day changes weather change first expanding tree buds + emerging leaves bird activity + nesting squirrel behavior flower emergence sequence in planted gardens
June·July·Aug. SUMMER	sequence of vegetable + flower gardens' growth configuration of the stars night sounds and smells varieties of insects + where found bird activity animal activity – rabbit·skunk etc tree + shrub varieties	animal activities – nesting· territorial defense· feeding varieties of grasses·sedges + rushes + their flowers celestial events habits of nesting birds reptiles + amphibians weather patterns what are first signs of fall?	activity of insects + where found conifer + deciduous varieties zonation of plants up a hillside or streambed birds + their nests life under a log or stone night activities of animals what happens to animals during a rainstorm?	flowering wild plants in vacant lots + along streets local bird activity temperature + weather charting insect evidence + sounds squirrel·raccoon·skunk or bat activity tree varieties along the streets what blooms in summer?
Sept·Oct·Nov. FALL	last summer flowers to bloom what leaves turn + fall first – why? sequence of bird departure weather changes night sounds + smells first frost migration observations of birds + other animals	insect activity – spiders animal preparations for winter when do grasses die back first frost's effects weather patterns bird activity what hibernates + what migrates + what dies?	preparations of animals for winter ripening seeds, nuts, berries location of mushrooms – what kinds? sequence of leaves turning night sky first snowfall what hibernates + what dies + what migrates small landscape studies	winter animal preparations – squirrels·starling flocks etc. sequence of flowers to fade last leaves to fall on what trees? first signs of frost – what dies night sounds – crickets + birds in migration weather changes + sequence of daylight diminishing
Dec·Jan·Feb. WINTER	temperature + weather chart activity of birds – at feeders animal tracks in snow + mud who eats what seeds + fruits small landscape studies ice patterns in lakes, ponds, streams night sky + position of stars rainy day activities outdoors	winter weeds landscape studies night walk – stars + sounds animal tracks + homes varieties of winter colors snowflake shapes tree silhouette contrasts tree bud shapes end of winter signs	animal tracks in snow animal activity – rodents, deer, skunk, raccoon, fox where snow accumulates most weather patterns – clouds varieties of evergreen trees resident birds – what doing? lichens + fungi – who eats them? animal homes – holes + nests	activities of birds + other animals – house sparrows, pigeons etc. tree silhouette varieties lengthening of daylight + its effect on animal activity winter weeds in vacant lots temperature + weather changes where snow accumulates most tree bud shapes

* Subjects to study in a field journal = add your own ideas & habitats *

Figure 3.16
Chart of suggested subjects to study during particular seasons and in particular environments. Adjust it to your own area and interests. Do not be limited by this list, but use it as a base and add to it.

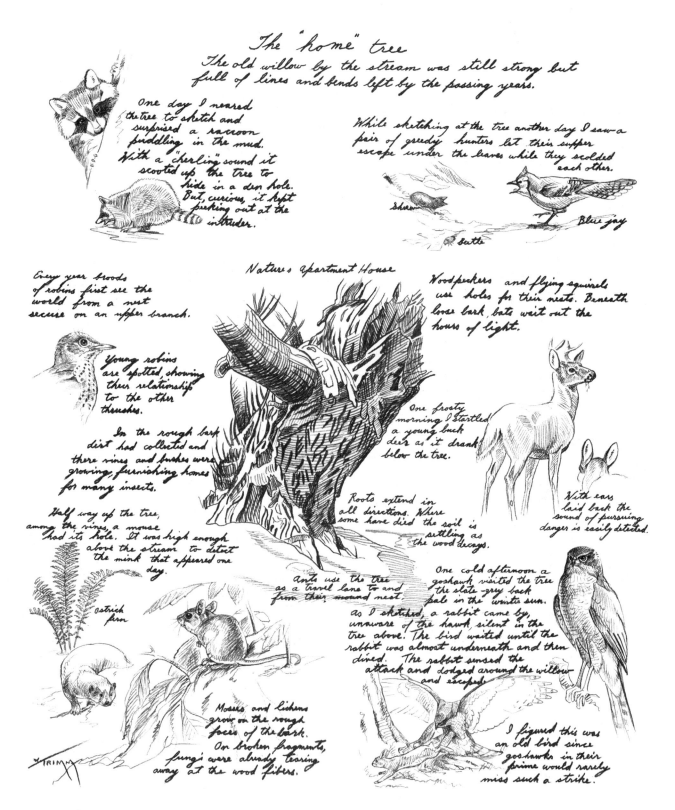

The "home" tree

The old willow by the stream was still strong but full of lines and bends left by the passing years.

One day I neared the tree to sketch and surprised a raccoon puddling in the mud. With a "cherling" sound it scooted up the tree to hide in a den hole. But, curious, it kept peeking out at the intruder.

While sketching at the tree another day I saw a pair of greedy hunters let their supper escape under the leaves while they scolded each other.

shrew
shrew
Blue jay

Nature's Apartment House

Every year broods of robins first see the world from a nest secure on an upper branch.

Young robins are spotted, showing their relationship to the other thrushes.

In the rough bark dirt had collected and there vines and bushes were growing, furnishing homes for many insects.

Half way up the tree, among the vines, a mouse had its hole. It was high enough above the stream to detect the mink that appeared one day.

Woodpeckers and flying squirrels use holes for their nests. Beneath loose bark, bats wait out the hours of light.

One frosty morning I startled a young buck deer as it drank below the tree.

With ears laid back the sound of pursuing danger is easily detected.

Roots extend in all directions. Where some have died the soil is settling as the wood decays.

ostrich fern

Ants use the tree as a travel lane to and from their mound nest.

One cold afternoon a goshawk visited the tree the slate-grey back pale in the winter sun. As I sketched, a rabbit came by, unaware of the hawk silent in the tree above. The bird waited until the rabbit was almost underneath and then dived. The rabbit sensed the attack and dodged around the willow and escaped.

Mosses and lichens grow on the rough faces of the bark. On broken fragments, fungi were already tearing away at the wood fibers.

I figured this was an old bird since goshawks in their prime would rarely miss such a strike.

Figure 3.17
"The home tree," a published sketchbook page by Wayne Trimm, artist from New York, art director, and senior editor of *The Conservationist*. Reprinted from The Conservationist, published by the New York State Department of Environmental Conservation with permission from the artist.

How habitat changes

WILDLIFE SKETCHBOOK

BY NED SMITH

WILDLIFE IS INEXORABLY keyed to plant succession. In many instances, animal numbers are merely a response to the changes in vegetation of its environment. For plants come and go. Abandoned fields are taken over by weeds, weeds are invaded by shrubs, and brushlands give way to encroaching forests. Each type of vegetation improves the site for the plants that will replace it. Correspondingly, each animal is displaced by a species better adapted to the new habitat.

An excellent example is an eastern mountain that has been devastated by a severe forest fire. For some time, the bare soil — scorched by flame and robbed of its humus — supports little but lichens, mosses and the toughest of grasses. Then, as bits of plant debris enrich the ashy dust, more plants become established. Pilewort and fireweed spring from windborne seeds. Passing birds sow pokeweed and blueberries with their droppings. Fallen leaves build more humus and, when the soil is receptive, drifting seeds of aspen establish the first trees. In the ensuing years a forest begins to grow. Not like the original forest, to be sure, for the rich soil that nurtured those trees will not be replaced for centuries, if then. But less demanding species will cover the scars and add their leaves to the soil accumulating beneath them. In time they will be replaced by trees of other species — a stable and self-perpetuating climax forest — and, at least in theory, plant succession will have come to an end.

Shortly after a fire, the dearth of vegetation is reflected in the paucity of animal life. But as plants gain a foothold, so do the insects that feed on them, and the birds that eat the insects. As cover improves, meadow mice find places to tunnel and feed, and weasels find good hunting.

A NIGHTHAWK LAYS ITS EGGS ON FIRE-BARED STONES AND CATCHES WANDERING MOTHS. THE FLICKER LEAVES ITS NEST HOLE IN A CHARRED SNAG TO LAP UP ANTS WHERE LICHENS AND A FEW GRASSES HAVE GAINED A FOOTHOLD.

SEEDS CARRIED BY THE WIND

MORE SOIL PRODUCES LUSH HERBACEOUS GROWTH, ATTRACTING BIRDS LIKE THE FIELD SPARROW (ABOVE) WHICH NEST AND FEED IN WEEDY PLACES.

WHEN BRUSH SUPPLANTS WEEDS FIELD SPARROWS AND MEADOW MICE GIVE WAY TO CARDINALS AND WHITE-FOOTED MICE. COTTONTAILS THRIVE IN DENSE SHRUB COVER.

Figure 3.18
Sketchbook pages occasionally appear in magazines to illustrate articles, such as this one done by wildlife illustrator Ned Smith for *National Wildlife*, a magazine of the National Wildlife Federation.
Reproduced courtesy of the artist.

Chapter 4
Sketching
Around the Home

Although the natural world is often spoken of in terms of rural or wilderness areas, it also exists within most human environments, even among those seemingly devoid of nature. It may appear in abundance in a carefully tended backyard or in a few spots adjacent to a city parking lot. But wherever one is outdoors, a stray weed, a bird, a clump of grass, or an insect can soon be found. And putting them in the context of the local landscape or environment, will help us to know more about our own living spaces.

Much of the awareness that plants, animals or birds share in our lives depends on a learned sensitivity to their presence. We may have a vague sense of birds singing beyond our window. But, usually, until someone points out that it is a blue jay, a cardinal, or a house sparrow, we drop the sound from our consciousness. There are many common, everyday events of nature right around our own homes if we know

where to look and what to look for. Historically, there have been numbers of renowned naturalists who rarely went beyond their own town to study all they wanted in the natural world. Of course, Thoreau is one of the best examples in this country.

Using the methods of field sketching, you can set up your own natural history study and learn a great deal about things that even the top scientists know little about. It is true that most scientists prefer to study more exotic species than the common robin hopping in their own back yard. I once asked an eminent entomologist from Harvard University about an interesting gray moth I had seen in my back yard, and he had no idea what it was or what its life history might be.

Do not feel, therefore, that you must go distances to draw and to observe nature. Many of us, due to pressures of time, jobs, or family have little opportunity for lengthy

The sketch contains the following handwritten labels: starling, elm tree, downy woodpecker, old fungus, marigolds + roses still in bloom + alyssum, crows chasing, E. napp, Squirrel pulling at something, Lydia, Nature in the November 9 2:20pm, city - a view from my desk

Figure 4.1a
While working on a drawing one day, I paused to look out the window.
Inspired by what was there, I got out my journal and using a felt-tipped pen
recorded briefly a moment observed in a city's landscape.

stretches of drawing or nature study. When we do have the time, we want our subjects readily available. This is precisely why both amateur and professional artist/naturalists turn to photographs or museum mounts for much of their resource material. Yet, the experience of seeing a subject in its own environment is vital if one is to have a full understanding of a larger ecological dynamic.

Edwin Way Teale was a naturalist/ writer who, although traveling throughout the country to write some of his books, spent many of his years studying his own

Figure 4.1b
Figure 4.1a was the inspiration for this illustration which appeared on the back
page of *Sanctuary*, the Massachusetts Audubon Society's newsletter, in January
1982. The intention of this sketch was to show the variety of nature subjects
that can be seen from a city window on an ordinary day, and to show the
subjects engaged in common activities.

plot of land in Connecticut. He wrote a
book about the seasons which guided my
own early observations of nature. In *Circle
of The Seasons: The Journal of a Naturalist's
Year* (Dodd, Mead, and Co., New York,
1953) Teale wrote in the last entry of
December 31:

There is, in nature, a timelessness, a
sturdy, undeviating endurance. . . . All
around us are the inconstant and the
uncertain. The institutions of men alter
and disintegrate. . . . But in the endless
repetitions of nature—in the recurrence of
spring, in the lush new growths that

replace the old, in the coming of new birds to sing the ancient songs, in the continuity of life and the web of the living—here we find the solid foundations that, on this earth, underlies at once the past, the present and the future.

It was Teale who showed me how to look at goldenrod galls, praying mantises, rain on leaves, earthworms, and red-winged blackbirds. He taught me not to take any of it for granted. Although he is a writer and I am an artist, we both have the same desire to record the miraculous in the most ordinary of events. You can do the same by just looking out your window or by taking no more than a five-minute walk around your yard.

Figure 4.2
Observational notations of house sparrow behavior that were drawn from the same desk window. These brief periods of watching add up. I have been seeing this pair (or a similar pair) of sparrows go through their various displays for three years now. One of the many things I have learned is that house sparrows mate throughout the year, begin fussing with their nests as early as January, but do not breed or rear young until spring.

Before you try drawing what you see, do some background work first. Establish whether you wish to use a field journal method as described in Chapter 3, a notebook where drawings and sketches will be interspersed among written notes on lined paper, or a drawing pad where sketches will predominate over writing. Establish *why* you want to study the landscape around your home, *what* your goals are, and *who* you are doing it for. Remember, we all do our best learning when we feel in control of our own education. Always try to balance the emphasis of improving your drawing with improving your observation skills.

Figure 4.3
These were sketched while looking principally at the animals and not at the paper. Shading and detail were refined from memory when the animal moved. It is important to keep the pencil moving and not to wait for the animal to regain a previous pose. Go on to fill up a page with five or six sketches of various shifting postures.

Again, before setting out to draw your backyard kingdom, become familiar with its general characteristics. Make a list of what might be found there and then add on to it as you discover new things and as the seasons change. You may live in the country, the city, in the woods, by a lake, in a suburb, or in a college dormitory. No matter where you live you need only to look out a window to draw cloud formations, positions of the sun, moon, or stars, contrasting varieties of trees and shrubs, a small sketch of the land's configuration, or perhaps a passing bird, insect or other animal. (See the chart, Figure 3.16 in Chapter 3 for specific subjects to look for by season and by habitat.)

Title your lists with the name of your street, town, and state. Record the date and year so that your list will have a seasonal as well as specific time focus. Then, space out eight categories on one or two sheets of

Figure 4.4
CLARE WALKER LESLIE
Studies of a dead chickadee drawn with HB and 3B pencils and watercolor wash. Take advantage of opportunities to draw fresh-killed animal, so that you may know better what it looks like when alive. This is helpful particularly as fur color fades once a specimen has been dead for any length of time.

white feathers
with black bases
so that underneath
is dark

gray

ochre

gray/
olive back

2 3 4
joints

19

12

white
stripe
on edge
of some

CWL
black-capped chickadee
12-27-82

paper. Label them as follows: Deciduous and Evergreen Trees, and Shrubs; Native Plants; Garden Plants; Birds; Mammals; Other Animals (reptiles, amphibians, insects); Geology; Weather. Somewhere on the page briefly describe your home landscape, such as—housing development in a mid-atlantic state's rolling foothill, single family home surrounded by oak/pine woods in a suburban community, or campus dormitory having only landscaped planting.

Go either to a window or outside your building. Become an explorer in the environment that you supposedly know best. See how many things you can notice

Figure 4.5
Described here is an unusual interchange, and one that brought up some yet unanswered questions: Why do sharp-shins chase blue jays? Why do blue jays chase sharp-shins? Why such displays of aggression so late in the season? Often when least expecting it some interesting events can be observed.

that you never knew were there before and list them under your categories. What is the insect on the rose bush, and what might it be doing? What plants grow next to the sidewalk? Is there any bird activity in the trees overhead? Stop for a moment and listen. Even if you do not know what they are, jot down a brief description of them using words and images. (See Figures 3.1 or 4.4.) Learning to listen, to smell, to touch, as well as to look carefully are essential components in becoming a good field sketcher. Bend over and see what is in the grass at your feet. There is a kingdom among the ant hills, the insect pathways, and the animal burrows. Go later to a field guide to learn what you have seen, but do not be too concerned with the names of things while you are outdoors. It is more important to watch what they are doing or how they are growing.

Outside our apartment in Cambridge, Massachusetts we have a Norway maple tree which has little room to grow between the curb of the street and the sidewalk slabs. Year by year more of its branches die and fall to the ground. Yet, the tree has been a yearly home to nesting starlings, and has provided insect food for neighboring downy woodpeckers, chickadees, a brown creeper. It has provided the territory for the courtship activities of numerous house sparrows, and has offered its top branches as excellent sentinel posts for several cardinals and blue jays in the spring when they have needed to sound off their spring calls. Without going ten feet from my home, I have learned a tremendous amount about bird behavior, much of which cannot yet be found in any literature about birds. Once you become an artist/naturalist of the "ordinary" events of nature, you will find that many of your questions may go unanswered. But this only adds to the mystery and interest in studying the natural world. (A helpful book on bird behavior is, *A Guide to the Behavior of Common Birds* by Donald W. Stokes. Little, Brown, and Company of Boston, 1979.)

Figure 4.6
While on the telephone I noticed a grey squirrel eating and then stuffing maple leaves into a maple tree hole. With a brown felt-tipped pen on a scrap of paper, I made note of what I saw. What was the squirrel doing? Was this to be its winter nest hole?

Sketching around the home can, in fact, allow you the most opportunity for observing nature on a daily basis. It is a place you know best and frequent most often. The seasonal cycle of trees on your lawn is comparable to the cycle of trees in the country. The activities of resident as well as migratory birds are similar, yet you will have a better opportunity to watch them on a regular basis, if you set up feeding stations, nesting boxes, or plant trees which attract birds. Although squirrels, chipmunks, rabbits, or skunks may not be what you have in mind for wildlife sketch-

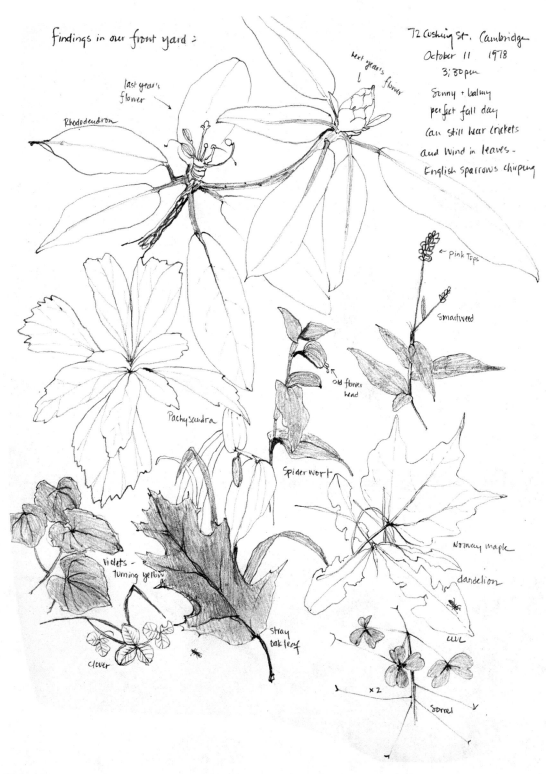

Figure 4.7
An interesting exercise can be one in which you draw the plants (and animals)
found within a designated space. The area could range in size from 3' x 3' up
to 30' x 30', but not much larger or the project takes on a different scope. This
project was done in the small yard in front of a city apartment. Until sitting
down to sketch, I had never noticed all that had been growing there.

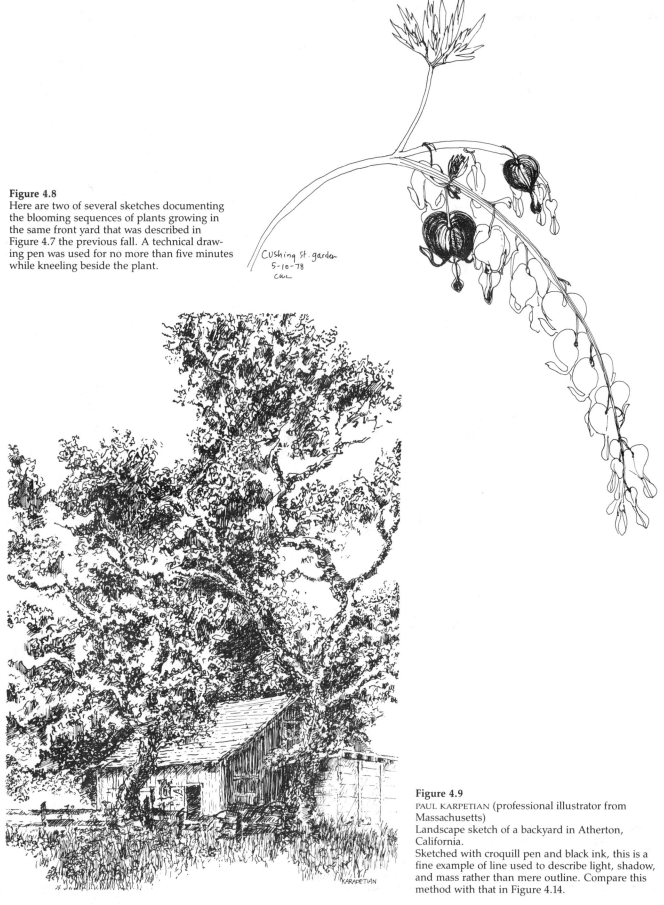

Figure 4.8
Here are two of several sketches documenting the blooming sequences of plants growing in the same front yard that was described in Figure 4.7 the previous fall. A technical drawing pen was used for no more than five minutes while kneeling beside the plant.

Cushing St. garden
5-10-78
cwc

Figure 4.9
PAUL KARPETIAN (professional illustrator from Massachusetts)
Landscape sketch of a backyard in Atherton, California.
Sketched with croquill pen and black ink, this is a fine example of line used to describe light, shadow, and mass rather than mere outline. Compare this method with that in Figure 4.14.

ing, they will, however be better subjects than a bobcat, fox, or deer, as they can be seen living close to human habitation and their activities can be observed for longer periods of time. I recommend to all students, that they spend time drawing their own cat or dog, guinea pig, gerbil, or the squirrels or chipmunks they find in their own back yards. It is important to observe any animal in motion, how it walks or feeds, how its body is constructed, and how its fur lies along its body. Much can be learned from the common gray squirrel about how to draw other members of the rodent family, such as the muskrat, meadow mouse, flying squirrel, or beaver.

Figure 4.10
Stopping to watch a small event happening outdoors can make a day have more interest. I watched this pair for several weeks while I busied about with an active household. Reflecting on the adult phoebe's activity in comparison to mine, I realized they worked for longer hours than I did.

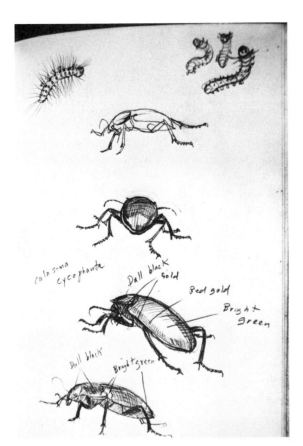

Figure 4.11
WAYNE TRIMM (professional wildlife artist from New York)
Soft-pencil field sketches of a beetle and a caterpillar.

Figure 4.12
When sketching snow, you need to place images *around* areas of paper to be left white. Watch to see where snow falls and how it changes the shapes of things as well as being changed itself by shadows and highlights.

Figure 4.13
GUNNAR BRUSEWITZ (Swedish artist/naturalist)
Study of an old mill in the snow (pencil with watercolor).
Small landscape sketches such as this can be done from a window or by
finding subjects not very far from home. Observe how the artist increases the
whiteness of the snow with strong contrasts of dark water, trees, and building.

If unable to take your sketch pad with you outdoors, make a clear mental note of something that you wish to record later when back indoors. Remember three or four key features and as soon as you can on return, jot a brief sketch of it in your journal or sketch pad. *Then*, go to a field guide or to photographs and redo a more accurate and detailed drawing or sketch so that you can better imprint into your mind exactly how the subject looked. Refer to the memory sketches reproduced in this book and to Exercise 3 in Chapter Two on memory sketching.

Observational sketching can also be done indoors if you are unable to be outside in a situation where you can do field sketching. Things collected from an outdoor walk, such as dried seed pods, grasses, mushrooms, twigs, or shells can be sketched on return. There is a tendency to want to make more extensive drawings, so try to limit your drawing time to approximately five minutes per object and shift the emphasis from creating a finished work to creating an informational sketch.

When sketching any subject, try to find something extraordinary about it, no matter how ordinary it may appear. Try to describe in your sketch what is interesting from both artistic as well as scientific points. Learn to ask questions that will lead to learning more about the subject. If drawing an acorn, for example, ask yourself why it is round; what is the function of the cap; are there differently shaped acorns; who eats them; why are they brown; when do they first appear on a tree; what are the seeds like on other neighboring trees. You can learn a great deal about oak trees, and botany in general, without going very far from home.

Figure 4.14
My grandfather, William H. Walker, was a professional artist who always kept a
sketchbook nearby. Perhaps this was a study for a painting or just something
that caught his eye. Notice his interest in light and shadow as it defines form.
He was an artist who used the full range of the pencil's tones.

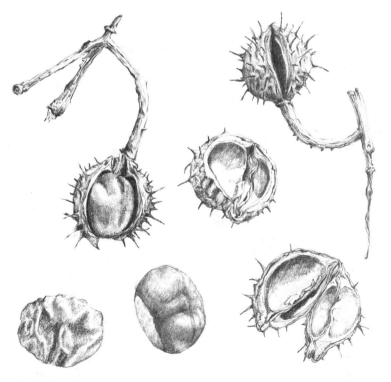

Figure 4.15
CARLA BRENNAN (artist from
Massachusetts)
Studies of horse chestnuts taken from
field journals.
Carla was studying form, tone, and
pencil technique, in addition to gathering
information about a horse chestnut.

Figure 4.16
Here are twigs collected from a walk and drawn once back indoors with a technical pen (I generally do not carry a good pen outdoors.) I was primarily interested in the contrasting shapes of these twigs, which were all collected from trees growing along our road. The drawings were entered later in my field journal when I had a quiet moment to study them.

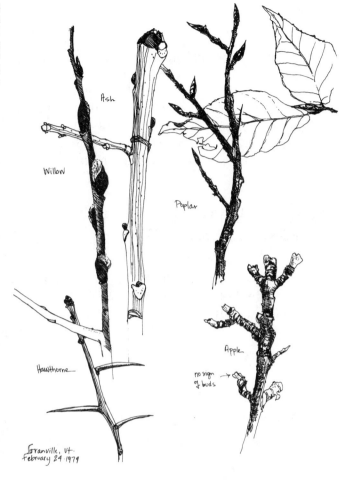

Ash

Willow

Poplar

Hawthorne

Apple

no sign of buds →

Granville, Vt.
February 24, 1979

gray brown fur
white under parts

approx. length 3½"
tail 3"

deer mouse

← bi-coloured tail

This is what leaves hazelnuts
in our bathroom floor,
rice in our coat pockets
+ barberry seeds
in our beds

7-12

Figure 4.17
If sketching recently-killed specimens, be sure to draw various angles to learn as much about features and shape as possible. Mark down necessary identification markings. (If you do not want to store a specimen in the refrigerator for later sketching, expect to have enough immediate time to do at least an hour's drawing series to get any real sense of the creature.)

Use the illustrations in this chapter as guides for exercises that you can do on your own or with a class. The following list gives general categories of locations around home where you can do field sketching. Add onto the list as you get to know your home area and your own interests.

SUGGESTED HABITATS FOR FIELD SKETCHING

In choosing where and what to sketch, special attention should be given to the fact that you want to describe not just a portrait of a place or thing, but a particular feeling or character if it is a landscape, and a particular behavior or physial feature if it is an animal or plant. When outdoors, you are studying an environment and its elements. There will be plenty of time when back inside to do more refined drawings.

- *Looking Out the Window:*
  Deciduous or evergreen tree and shrub shapes throughout the seasons; bird activity—feeding, roosting, preening, courting, nesting, "loafing", defending territory; weather, cloud formations, rain and snow, moon rise and sunset, stars and constellation configurations; small landscape

Figure 4.18
There are many wildlife programs on television today that are well worth a try at sketching. They offer terrific experience in drawing animals in their natural setting. Although highly challenging because the animals move rapidly and often disappear from view, the film simulates a real-life situation with the benefits of close observation and sequences of behavioral activities. Images can be reworked and improved upon during the commercials. Television sketching also provides an opportunity to learn about groups of animals in specific habitats, with educational narrative to help your sketching take on more meaning.

studies no larger than 3″ × 5″ to be varied according to the season; plants both wild and cultivated; presence of any wild or domestic animals.

- *Inside the Home:*
  Potted plants or cut flowers both from outdoors or from a florist; household pets in various poses of activity; objects collected from an outdoor walk to be sketched for identification; indoor insects such as house flies, an occasional beetle or ant; TV sketching of wildlife films.

- *Around the Yard:*
  Weed and grass varieties; seasonal plants in the flower and vegetable garden and their growth sequences; types of trees and shrubs—sketch their buds, flowers, seeds,

twigs, bark and overall shape; an ecological study by season of a backyard pond, stream, school yard, vacant lot or other nearby space that is no larger than an acre.

- *Neighborhood Conservation Land, Nature Center, Wildlife Sanctuary, or Park:*
  Observation of one specific area on a regular basis for several seasons to be recorded, if possible, in the journal format; landscape studies of specific environments, combining a small sketch of the landscape with sketches of the various plants and animals within it, all on the same page or on accompanying pages; study of specific plants throughout a year; observation of squirrel activity; sketching live animals and birds that are both caged and wild.

Figure 4.19
While studying wildflowers in a local nature center's garden, this toad hopped into view. (Done with a felt tipped pen.)

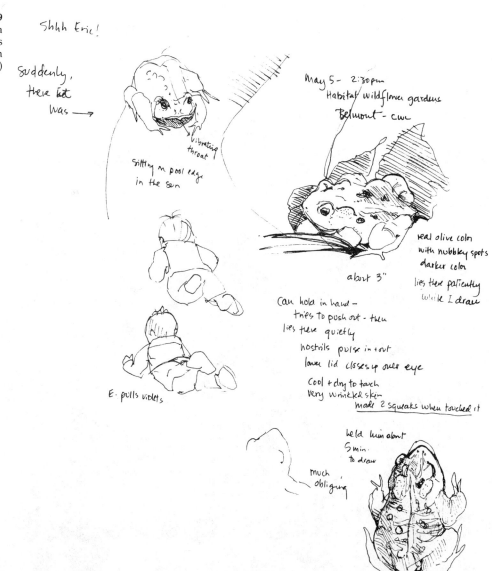

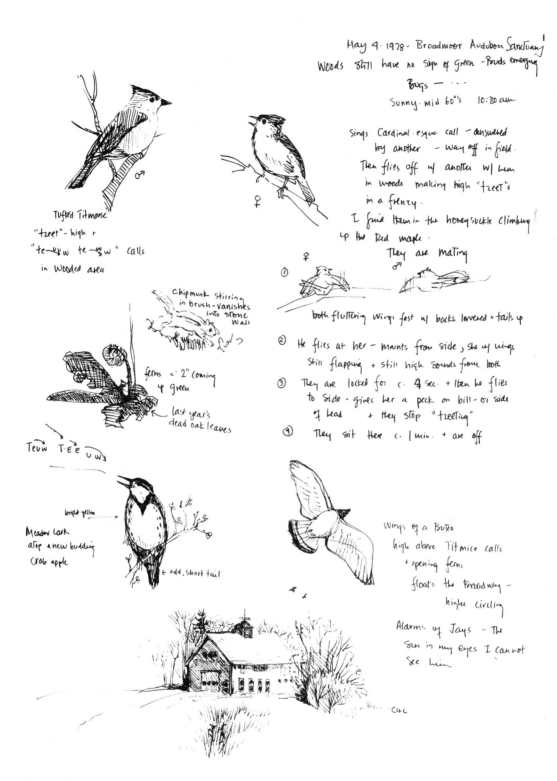

May 9 1978 - Broadmoor Audubon Sanctuary
Woods still have no sign of Green - Fronds emerging
Bugs — ...
Sunny mid 60°'s   10:30 am

Sings Cardinal-esque call - answered
by another - way off in field.
Then flies off w/ another w/ him
in woods making high "tzeet"s
in a frenzy.
I find them in the honeysuckle climbing
up the Red maple.
♀   They are mating   ♂

① both fluttering wings fast w/ backs lowered + tails up

② He flies at her - mounts from side, she w/ wings
still flapping + still high sounds from both

③ They are locked for c. 4 sec + then he flies
to side - gives her a peck on bill - or side
of head   + they stop "tzeeting"

④ They sit there c. 1 min. + are off

Tufted Titmouse
"tzeet"- high r
"te-w̌ w te-w̌ w" calls
in Wooded area

Chipmunk stirring
in brush - Vanishes
into stone wall

ferns c. 2" coming
up green

last year's
dead oak leaves

Teuw TĒE uw

bright yellow
Meadow Lark
atop a new budding
crab apple

odd, short tail

Wings of a Buteo
high above Titmice calls
+ opening ferns
floats the Broadwing -
high circling

Alarms of Jays - The
Sun in my eyes I cannot
see him

caw

Figure 4.20
One spring, I visited a local Audubon sanctuary weekly to observe and record
as much as possible in a morning's walk. I went without expectation of what
might be found and began the day by walking slowly along a path for about
fifteen minutes, trying to be fully aware of what was immediately around. Soon
something would rustle in the leaves or fly overhead, and I would be off on a
morning's investigation, recording whatever came along. As you can see, it was
nothing spectacular, and yet, it was very much so. My focus was to observe the
progression of spring in its various states of animal and plant activity. I learned
a great deal of local natural history during this period. For example, I had never
taken the time to watch titmouse courtship before.

Drumlin Farm Nature Centre,
Lincoln, Mass.
Sunday, 1st Febuary, 1981.
~ 37°F.

× ⅓

Hoof print
in the snow

Operated by the Mass.
Audubon Society, Drumlin
Farm (220-acres) includes
pasture, fields, woodland,
ponds, and both domestic
and wild animals.

As with all
deer, only the
buck has antlers.

white bottom
lip and neck
patch.

Tail edged
with white:
when deer
is alarmed or
in flight it
lifts tail into
vertical position
exposing
large white area
on rump and
underside of tail

An attempt to better
understand proportion and
perspective by emphasizing
geometric shapes.
— head is
drawn too
large.

WHITE-TAILED
DEER.

(odocoileus
virginianus).

Winter behaviour:
1) Generally bed down during
   the day. Bedding area must
   be warm and protected from sight.
2) Feed at night: buds of
   deciduous trees and foliage
   of evergreens.
3) Stay within a limited
   area, and pack trails within
   it to help get through deep
   snow and to escape predators.

Quickly lifts head and flexs ears
when disturbed during feeding

Figure 4.21
STEVE LINDELL (British research chemist)
Field studies of white-tailed deer.
Ken Carlson, a prominent American wildlife artist, comments in Patricia van
Gelder's book *Wildlife Artists at Work*, "Through observation you get a feeling
about how the animals should look and how they behave, which cannot be
captured even by a photo . . . . I sketched for years at the zoo to learn how an
animal moves" (pp. 38 and 47).

Figure 4.22

CLARE WALKER LESLIE

Studies of a red fox in Weyehill, England, 1976.

One summer I was fortunate enough to study with the well-known British wildlife artist, Dr. Eric Ennion. I drew the fox while Dr. Ennion sat beside me, also drawing. This is by far the best way to learn from a teacher. I have made an arrow pointing to the pencil line drawn in the lower right corner. Ennion spoke continually of hard and soft lines that give the impression of tone and mass without needing to add shading. He had us using 5B and 6B pencils, which, if sharpened with a knife, can form a variety of edges to the lead. The other arrow in the center of the page points to a shape that was first drawn and then shaded in as one manner of blocking out tonal areas. (This technique is used by a number of wildlife artists, one being Francis Lee Jacques, as illustrated in Figure 6.21) Another point Dr. Ennion repeatedly spoke of was, "Do not make a pretty picture but draw what you see . . . Get the major features that say *fox.*" He was a master in evoking the essence of an animal's character with the minimum of lines and color. At 76 Ennion had many years of study behind him yet he forever gave the impression he was still learning.

Figure 4.23
CLARE WALKER LESLIE
Studies of Canada geese at
Massachusetts Audubon Society's
Drumlin Farm, 1982. 3B technical pencil.
Observe the emphasis upon recording
specific behavioral postures.

Figure 4.24
When drawing animals, you never know
when they might get up and wander off.
Therefore, a very rapid line placement
(the gesture method) sets in the general
pose and shape. If the animal moves, the
basic form has already been defined. If
the animal remains, more detail can be
applied until you decide you have done
enough or the animal moves. This 2B
pencil sketch of a neighbor's dog took
about five minutes.

Chapter 5

Sketching Nature in the City

Despite what one may think, the city offers a great opportunity to study and sketch nature. Nature has conditioned itself to survive despite the challenges made daily upon it by the human environment. Perhaps it is due to the sharp contrast with brick, asphalt, and urban congestion that plants, animals, and birds stand out in keen relief against a city's background.

I often surprise people when I say that I see more varieties of nature in the city than in the country. One reason for this is that the flora and fauna that exist in the city concentrate themselves in small green areas, which can be as big as a park or as small as a crack in a sidewalk. On the other hand, in the country, birds and animals can range over large areas, and herbacaeous and woody plants do not come in such assortments. This is due to the fact that in the city most species have been planted, and many are not native but have been

imported because they grow well in urban conditions. For example, marigolds, which are native to Mexico, thrive in the city but cannot be found growing wild in the country. Other imports to our cities are the French horse chestnut, the Japanese maple, the English hawthorn, and the Chinese gingko. Among the birds imports include the English house sparrow and the European starling. Many urban parks, backyard gardens, and even borders around office buildings can have patches of spring bulbs, evergreen shrubs, and summer-flowering annuals, all of which, because they are from nursery stock, do not grow wild in the country. A lesson in urban natural history is a lesson in the colonization of its peoples; for, when a city is settled, its people bring along memories from the homeland—favored plants that then adjust, too, to the new world. A walk down a city street today can be a walk into parts of an old English

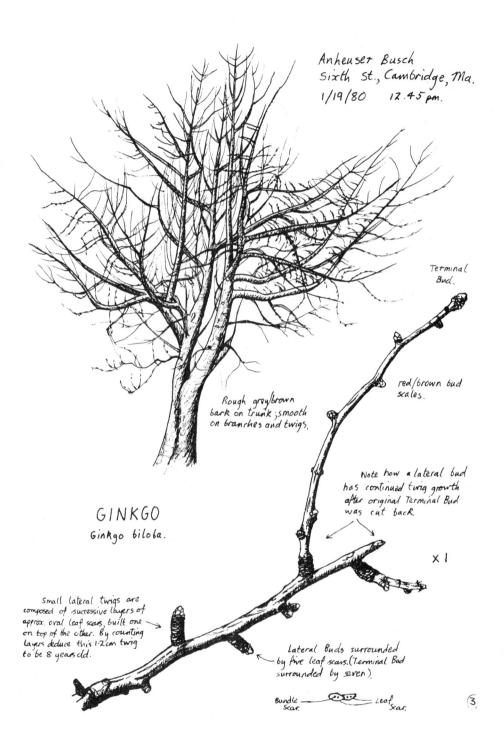

Anheuser Busch
Sixth St., Cambridge, Ma.
1/19/80   12.45 pm.

Terminal
Bud.

red/brown bud
scales.

Rough grey/brown
bark on trunk; smooth
on branches and twigs.

Note how a lateral bud
has continued twig growth
after original Terminal Bud
was cut back

GINKGO
Ginkgo biloba.

×1

Small lateral twigs are
composed of successive layers of
approx. oval leaf scars, built one
on top of the other. By counting
layers deduce this 1·2 cm twig
to be 8 years old.

Lateral Buds surrounded
by five leaf scars.(Terminal Bud
surrounded by seven).

Bundle ____   ____ Leaf
Scar.   Scar.

③

Figure 5.1
STEVE LINDELL
Field journal page.
A former student of mine, Steve used his journal as a means of studying the
new area where he was living.

garden; for one can find pepperweed, cocklebur, speedwell, heal-all, Queen Anne's Lace and many more.

Another factor that accounts for the abundance of species in the city relates to the climate. Due to the warmth transmitted by hot streets and buildings, spring comes earlier, and fall stays later. When all the leaves are off the trees just ten miles out into the country, a number of trees still hold leaves in the city. Also, several wild animals have found their way into urban regions. Due to food availability from open trash barrels and litter on the streets, raccoons, oppossum, rats, house mice, gray squirrels and occasional rabbits and red fox find city living easier than in the country.

As I write, in my city apartment, I look out to see herring gulls gliding and turning in the sky just above. By watching for just a few moments, I can study the various poses they are taking and wonder about what they are doing. Why has that one just flipped? What are they looking for? Where have they come from? How can I tell they are herring and not another type of gull? It is from brief observations such as these that you can begin your study of nature in the

Figure 5.2
A landscape sketch can provide one way of listing various trees and plants on a given piece of property. Notice how labels have been added to the trees, whereas in a less diagnostic type of landscape study this would not be done. Actually labelling plants in a sketch can be most useful for landscape designers or architects.

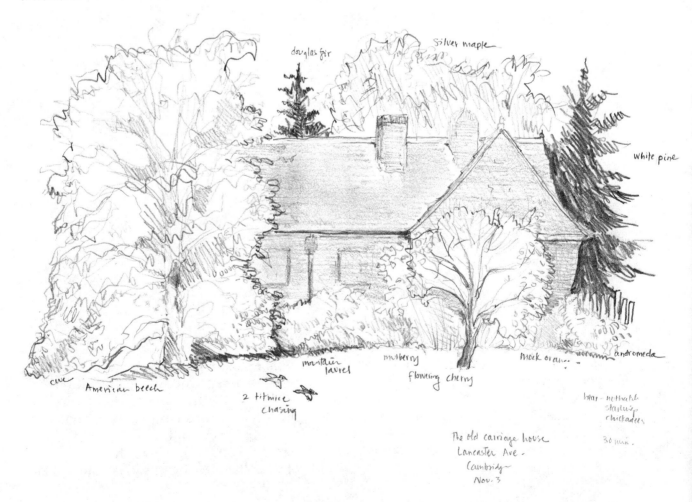

A student drawing in a class at the Busch Reisinger museum, Cambridge
10-27-82
10:30 am
Sunny, 50's
Ground wet from yesterday's
pigeons
Boston ivy leaves now red
blue berries
attaches by suckers
Spider webs on climbing rose
hosta
and peonies
fading violet leaves
bittersweet-climbing on walls
yellowed elm leaf on path
daisy fleabane still in bloom

Figure 5.3
Another identification sketch done in about thirty minutes' time. 2B pencil in a sketchbook.

city. Nature study does not have to be a big production. Much can be seen while on your way to work, while pausing to look out the window during a coffee break, or on a weekend stroll through the park. And likewise, the field sketches of these observations can be simple and without much technical detail.

In both spring and fall, a surprising number of migratory as well as resident birds, can be found in city arboretums and parks, and along riverways. From their flight above urban tracts, they spot these strips of green and will congregate for a rest, knowing that where there are masses of trees there are insects to be found. Many

Figure 5.4
Getting out of the car one rainy, misty day, I caught sight of a brilliant cluster of orange crocuses beside our apartment. Before going inside I did a brief study using felt-tipped pen and adding some colored pencil. If you carry a sketchbook in the car, you can take advantage of opportunities like this to draw.

sketch animals, gray squirrels, for example, are excellent subjects because they usually are found wherever there are groups of large trees where they can build their nests and be protected. Since they are so accustomed to people, they can often be enticed by peanuts or bread, and so sketched from close distances. Behavior activities can be easily studied throughout the year with a squirrel. There is much time spent in open food-hunting, courtship or defense of territory-chasing, nest-building, and rearing of young. Two broods of young may be produced, in late winter and in late spring. Learning to draw the common gray squirrel will help you to draw other mammals in the rodent (gnawing mammal) fam-

Figure 5.5
Finding it so unusual to see a barred owl settled in a tree beside this busy city street, I pulled an envelope out of my purse and on the back briefly sketched proof that this had been seen on a chilly night in November. People who stopped wondered what I was sketching before they looked up.

birdwatchers go not just to the countryside in spring, but to these green oases where they may be assured of seeing such birds as parula, palm, and Wilson's warblers or blue-winged teal, pintails, and ruddy ducks. An avid birdwatcher in Boston once wrote an article with a list of birds he had seen over the past ten years from his office in a large building complex in the heart of the city. His list of about sixty birds included the great blue heron, black duck, peregrine falcon, Canada geese, and white-throated sparrow. Perhaps because many birdwatchers happen to live in the city lists such as this one are not all that unusual.

An interesting aspect about studying nature in the city is that there are fewer places for animals to hide or for plants to blend in within a larger mass of vegetation. The species that exist are usually readily seen or heard. If first learning to field

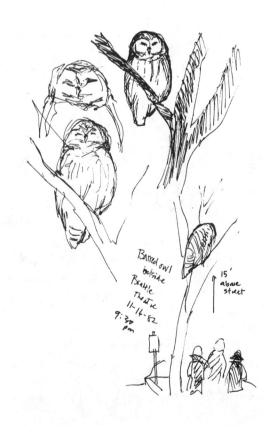

An Eric-nap drawing
4:30 pm
May 6
Mount Auburn Cemetery

Figure 5.6
Having drawing equipment in the car meant I could sketch while giving our son a nap. Cemeteries or parks with roadways are good places to go when only able to sketch from a car window.

ily. In addition, it is thrilling to know that although these animals are citified, they are still wild and have wild ways about them that are comparable to those of relative species in the woods and far off prairies. Most libraries have books on the life of the gray squirrel with good photographs which can be drawn from. Get in the practice of first doing observational field sketches to familiarize yourself with the animal alive, and *then* go to a reference source for a more detailed study and finished drawing. Never try to do a finished drawing while watching something or you will waste a great deal of time looking at the paper and not at what is

in front of you. The wildlife British artist, Eric Ennion, whom I studied with said, "When in doubt always look and draw later. Learn to build up your powers of observation as well as your drawing powers."

Other animals that can be easily found and sketched on a regular basis in the city are birds. House sparrows, pigeons, starlings, and occasionally robins, downy woodpeckers, and blue jays can be found feeding, roosting, nesting, rearing young, or just flying about through the many urban neighborhoods. When possible, put out a bird feeder or acquaint yourself with a

FLIGHT MOVEMENTS

PIGEON: WMY
FLIGHT STUDY

Figure 5.7
WILLIAM M. YENKEVICH (professional illustrator from Pennsylvania) Sketches of pigeons. Bill remarked in a letter, "I know how I am with my field sketchbook. It's a kind of bible to me. It gives me so much needed information for my scientific illustrations and paintings, something the mind cannot hold." Personal communication, December 1982.

November 19 – a low 60°'s – to high 40°'s – Sunny day.
    A chance to enjoy one of those last warm + sparkley days –
Eric, Ann Gamble + I went to Fresh Pond at 2 pm, with binoculars and saw :

lesser scaup

Crystal light for seeing colors + forms clearly

pair of Goldeneye with them

4 ♂
3 ♀

a stunning array of Canvasback –
rust of necks glistening

black-throated green warbler in fall plumage

olive green

ruddy duck in winter plumage

kept diving

mockingbird chortling calls

black duck at water's edge under low shrubs of alder

Crows chasing in + out of willows – black silhouettes

white breasts glistening in the light

Figure 5.8
If you have not carried a sketchbook with you on a walk, make careful mental notes of what you observe and record it on return. Most of the page was sketched from memory with some reference help from a field guide, and entered in my journal. City reservoirs are good places in which to look for ducks and gulls, particularly in winter because they congregate where the water remains open.

particualr area that attracts several birds on a regular basis. Keep a seasonal journal of activity and you will learn perhaps as much as a university ornithologist can tell you about the habits of the "common" birds.

Wherever there is planting in the city, there are insects to be found. Honey and bumble bees as well as ants and wasps climb over the most urbanized flowers. One can find spiders stringing webs from street signs, monarch butterflies darting past an office window, or even a dragon fly landing on a car while waiting at a stop light. Once

while paying for a book over the counter of a store I watched a beetle slowly wend its way across the cash register. Fortunately, the cashier never was told and I went out smiling at the amusing way nature makes its way into the human world. Upon returning home, I went right to a guide book to find out what it was, but I never found out how it got there or what it was doing.

As suggested in Chapter 4, first lay out a chart or list of the natural subjects that you have noticed around your apartment building, office, single family home, or along your commute to work or school. If you find you can think of very little, take a pad with you on the next commute or go now to a window and list what you see. Try to fill in three or four subjects under each of the eight categories (of course this will vary by season and by location): Deciduous and Evergreen Trees and Shrubs; Native Plants; Garden Plants; Birds; Mammals; Other Animals (Reptiles, Amphibians, Insects); Geology; Weather. Title your list with the address of your dwelling, or the district through which you commute, and the name of the city and state. Record a date and year so that your list will have a seasonal as well as specific time focus. Then, briefly describe the overall characteristics of the urban habitat which you will be studying. Is it predominantly residential? Are there front lawns and tended gardens? Is it mostly asphalt with apartment or office highrises? Does it include a park, or river, or lake front? What is the ratio of people to nature? Is it a small or large city? Is it in the East, Midwest, or Far West of this country? Having a list at the front of your journal or your sketch book will help you decide what specific elements you wish to observe and what elements seem to be most observable during certain seasons, on a given day, or even time of the day. Obviously, you will not be able to observe varieties of tree buds in summer or the rearing of starling young in winter.

Figure 5.9
Walking past one of Harvard's brick buildings one day, I chanced to see this insect hovering over the ivy covering the walls. On return, I looked in a guidebook and found it to be a day-flying moth and not a butterfly, as I had expected. Had I not accustomed myself over the past several years to be always on the look out for such interesting events as this one, I doubt I would have noticed the moth. It is true, the more you use your journal as a means of learning about nature, the more there will be to learn.

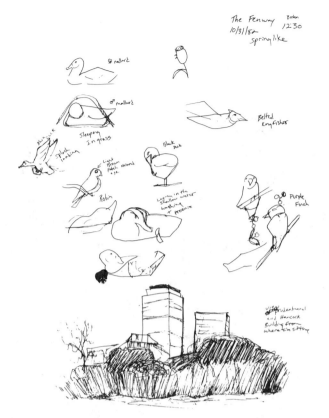

Figure 5.10
This field sketch was done by a student of mine currently enrolled at a local art college. He had never before sketched nature outdoors. Although humbled by the results, he was excited by what he had seen and by the fact it had given him opportunity to spend some time in a place he liked. He found himself sketching birds doing things that elicited numerous questions about bird behavior.

Figure 5.11
Small vistas can be sketched by going down to the river, to a park, or to any area where there is a bit of open space. Keep the drawings small and free of detail. Do not sketch for longer than thirty minutes to keep your drawings fresh and not overworked. Record place, date, and time so that you tie what you are drawing in to a particular time and seasonal reference. This sketch was done with a 2B and a 4B pencil within an 8" x 4" frame. For more information on landscapes refer to Chapter 2.

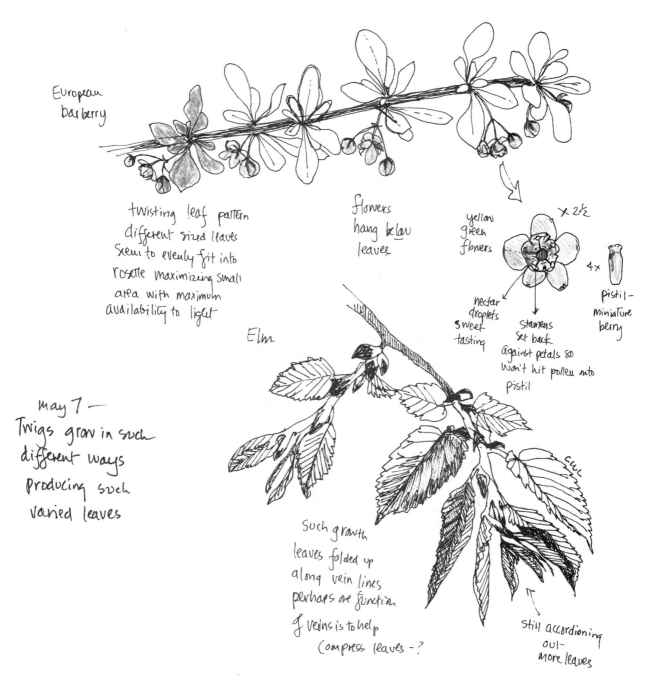

Wind pollinated flowers must have florets out exposed above leaves to catch the slightest drift. Insect pollinated more colorful + set close to leaves

So much flowering + leaf growth activity just in 2 weeks. Too much to keep up with — especially since a lot seems to be happening while it is raining

European barberry

twisting leaf pattern different sized leaves seem to evenly fit into rosette maximizing small area with maximum availability to light

Flowers hang below leaves

yellow green flowers

× 2½

nectar droplets sweet tasting

stamens set back against petals so won't hit pollen onto pistil

4×

pistil — miniature berry

Elm

may 7 — Twigs grow in such different ways producing such varied leaves

Such growth leaves folded up along vein lines perhaps one function of veins is to help compress leaves — ?

curl

still accordioning out — more leaves

Figure 5.12
I collected two twigs from our street to study more closely indoors because I was interested in learning about their leaf and floral structures. I used a technical pen with a bit of colored pencil, and drew this into my field journal.

Figure 5.13
The student who did these studies was more interested in the beauty of form than in scientific structure. Sketching serves both scientific and artistic purposes.

Figure 5.14
Sketching from a train window can present a real challenge but definitely makes the ride more interesting. Because you are constantly looking for things to draw, you become very aware of every detail that flashes by. I was quite surprised by the number of natural things we identified as we traveled through rather unattractive parts of metropolitan Boston.

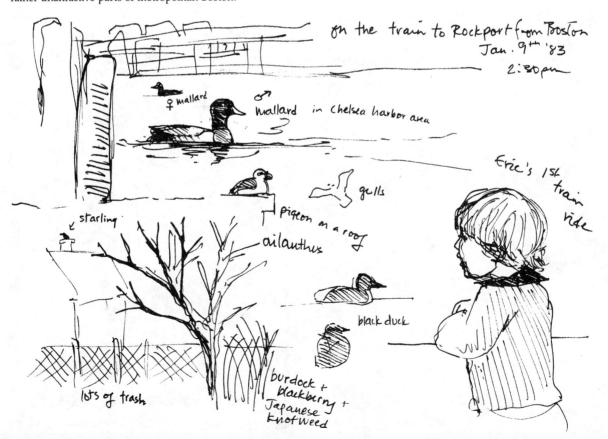

on the train to Rockport from Boston
Jan. 9th '83
2:30 pm

♀ mallard   ♂ mallard   in Chelsea harbor area

gulls

pigeon on a roof

starling

ailanthus

black duck

lots of trash

burdock + blackberry + Japanese knotweed

Eric's 1st train ride

City sketching of nature need not be done only outside. Zoos, aquariums, greenhouses, science museums, and university biology departments are important to frequent. There, animals and plants can be seen at close range and studied in ways that are not possible when encountered outdoors. Sketching, as a method of recording what is in a museum, can also provide a valuable way of taking notes without the necessity of staying for lengthy periods in front of a display. Limit yourself to ten minutes per note-taking sketch and you will not only speed up your powers of observation, but you will also be surprised at how much information you can record. Try to concentrate your studies on those animals or plants that are local to your region or to those you are likely to see outdoors. Although it is fun to draw tigers and elephants, if you are involved in a study of your own habitat and the animals within, you won't learn much from these animals that is relevant.

Figure 5.15
WILLIAM H. WALKER (American political cartoonist, 1871-1938)
Sketches of Polar Bears at the Bronx Zoo.
Zoos are excellent resources for sketching animals. Although not in their native habitats, you do have a chance to study features and postures at close range. All wildlife artists, at one time or another, go to zoos or other live animal centers; there they can make pages and pages of observational sketches and studies of particular features they may not have reference for from a photograph or other sketches done in the wild. Walker used these sketches in a political cartoon for *Life* magazine in 1904, in which Russia was represented by a bear.

Figure 5.16
BOB KUHN (contemporary wildlife painter)
Sketches of a cougar, brown conte crayon.
Reproduced by courtesy of the artist.

In his book *The Animal Art of Bob Kuhn*, (Connecticut: North Light Publishers, 1973, p. 13) Bob says of sketching: "Frequently, the quick indication of a gesture is all you can manage, and all you should attempt. You might decide to make a careful study of an animal's head, an arrangement of limbs, a paw or some other segment of the whole animal. It matters not. Nor does it matter too much if you mislay a sketchbook or two. The real gain is in your growing knowledge of your subject."

Figure 5.17

RICHARD GAYTON (professional illustrator from California)
Sketches of a black and white casqued hornbill from the San
Francisco Zoo done in Ko-i-noor's Negro pencil.

Figure 5.18

JOHN BUSBY (British artist)
Sketches of snowy owls in the Edinburg Zoo done in soft
pencil with watercolor wash.
Busby has a superb ability to convey the essence of a bird,
using a minimum of lines. This comes from many hours
spent sketching and watching birds outdoors. It is his
interest not to describe physical detail so much as the form
and character of the bird, as if from the inside out, as he
explains it. In my opinion, John is one of the great artists of
the field sketch today. In a letter to me he said, "using a
sketchbook keeps one's eye fresh . . . You are always
drawing from the bird itself. While the camera freezes the
movement in a moment in time, the sketch can give the *sense*
of movement by the selective use of line and emphasis on
detail" (Personal communication, November 1982)

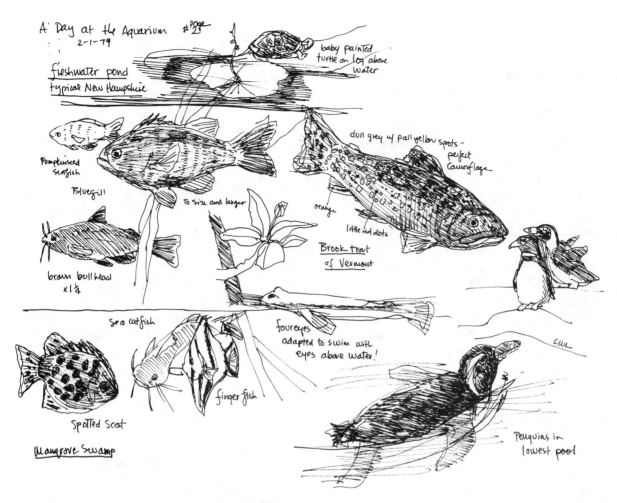

Figure 5.19

In the notes I took this day while sketching at the New England Aquarium in Boston, I wrote as though to my students, "First, look around and see what's there. Choose no more than three or four exhibits to sketch in a morning or no more than twenty minutes per exhibit. Be prepared for dim light, standing up awkwardly propping a pad, and sketching around crowds of people. Use a felt-tipped pen, since its dark lines are easier to see. Read labels to find out about the fish. If drawings accompany the dioramas, see how the fish are drawn there." These sketches were used simply to get my eyes looking and were not touched up later. The process of seeing/sketching, once again is more important than the produced drawing.

Figure 5.20

I use a felt-tipped pen a lot when quickly sketching or when away from my drawing table. I do this for several reasons. Since I cannot erase, I must look more carefully, and, the images often come out more crisply than when using pencil. Since I write many notes, the pen serves both purposes well. Also, I always have a pen somewhere with me, whereas I often forget my pencil case. But if you find pencil preferable, then use it. This sketch, done in a 5½" x 8½" spiral drawing pad that I carry when I travel, took no more than ten minutes and contains the information I wanted.

One advantage of living in an urban area is the accessibility to institutions for learning about nature when one is unable to go to nature directly. In fact, many of this country's great naturalists and naturalist/artists lived in cities, as this is where their employment was. The National Museum of Natural History, a part of the Smithsonian Institution is in Washington, D.C. The Academy of Natural Sciences is in Philadelphia. The American Museum of Natural History is located in New York City, and the Field Museum of Natural History is in Chicago. Excellent museums of natural history are also located in Cleveland, Minneapolis, Los Angeles, and San Francisco, among other cities.

A book that has helped increase my knowledge of urban nature and which has aided my students, is written by the naturalist/writer John Kieran who spent most of his life in New York City. His book is titled *A Natural History of New York City* (Houghton-Mifflin Company of Boston, 1959). Mr. Kieran is quoted on the jacket's fly leaf as saying:

> . . . the destruction or elimination of plant and animal life in the area, through the blanketing of the ground by buildings and pavements, is largely a matter of quantity, and not of kind . . . . The remaining one-fifth of the open ground or water will contain practically all the kinds of plant and animal life that once filled the whole area, but by no means the same quantity . . . There are more than 28,000 acres of public parkland within the city limit . . . . Let the population of the area increase and multiply as it may, let men build and pave to their heart's content, there will always be many kinds and untold numbers of wild things in the great city.

SUGGESTED HABITATS FOR SKETCHING NATURE IN THE CITY

Those of us who love nature, and yet must live in the cities due to jobs, schooling constraints, or families, can still find much to see in nature if we learn where to look.

Whether you use the journal/diary format, a small 3 × 5 sketch pad in a pocket, or a spiral drawing pad, try to do sketching on a regular basis, even if it can only be ten minutes, two times a week. Only by sketching regularly can you improve your technique, as well as document within a sequence the shifting of the seasons. Do *not* be concerned with the quality of your drawing. Technique can be worked on by drawing bowls of fruit, coffee cups, or a sleeping cat. Sketching demands that you record with accuracy of observation. Having done so, your method of drawing can only improve over time. Refer to the chart in Chapter 3 for a list of subject categorized by the season, which can be sketched in the city habitat.

- *Along city streets:*
  Sketch deciduous, or evergreen tree and shrub shapes throughout the seasons; bird activity—feeding, roosting, preening, courting, nesting, "loafing," defending territory; weather, cloud formations, rain and snow, moon rise and sunset, stars and constellations. Do small landscape studies no larger than 3" × 5" to be varied according to the season. Sketch plants, both wild and cultivated. Watch for the presence of any wild or domestic animals (squirrels, rats or mice, raccoon, skunk, bats, insects, cats, dogs).

- *Collecting and sketching at home:*
  Gather small branches from trees, flowering plants, seeds or nuts from trees and shrubs, feathers, shells, stones, grasses.

- *While commuting on the train, bus, or by car:*
  Sketch small landscapes, tree shapes, flowers in bloom, bird activity, neighborhood landscape contrasts. Inventory how much of nature can be found in differing neighborhoods.

- *In an outdoor park, small garden, cemetery, or arboretum:*
  Sketch small landscapes, tree shapes, flowers in bloom, bird activity, herbaceous plants both wild and cultivated, weed vari-

eties, local animals (mammals and insects in particular).

- *In a backyard or front yard:*
  Sketch small landscapes, tree shapes, flowers in bloom, bird activity, herbaceous plants both wild and cultivated, weed varieties, local animals (mammals and insects in particular).

- *At a zoo:*
  Do sketches of varying poses of animals, particularly those from your region. Do one-minute, five-minute, and thirty-second sketches and then one ten-minute drawing to work on your technique. Emphasize learning movement and behavior in your sketches and details of form in your drawing.

- *At the aquarium:*
  Use methods of sketching to learn fish types and their habitat groupings.

- *At the science museum or natural history museum:*
  Use a variety of methods, with both pen and pencil, to record what interests you in the museum. Do small landscape studies at the dioramas and do several animals within a family grouping in the display cases. Contrast methods of sketching with a few drawings.

- *At the university biology department:*
  Sketching is to be used here to gather as much information as you can about a species; combine drawing with writing methods and try to be as scientific about your observation as possible. Have a scientist review your sketches for accuracy.

- *At a flower show or botanical museum:*
  Document what you see by sketching for later reference or for describing more fully to someone else what you saw. A sketch well done can speak better than many words.

Chapter 6
Sketching in the Country

A trip into the countryside can be even more interesting if you take along a sketchbook. There are numerous ways to use drawing to record what you are seeing, as the illustrations in this chapter suggest. You may wish to use it as a way of learning about a particular habitat, by making frequent sketching forays to one chosen place and throughout several seasons. You may wish to use it in conjunction with birdwatching or you may wish to use it as a form of nature diary while on vacation. Take some time to think about what it is about a specific habitat that interests you and then study it by recording your observations.

Sketching allows opportunities to take another look at habitats that are quite diverse and to examine closely what properties make one distinct from another, such as open pasture land from deciduous or evergreen woodland, sandy beach from rocky coast, northern hardwood forest from southern hardwood forest or midwestern prairie from southwest desert. Throughout the world there are different regions that are defined by various ecological components having universal components. A rocky coast in Norway bears resemblance to a rocky coast in Maine. American farmland bears resemblance to British farmland. The deserts of this country have features like those in Africa. Find literature to read about the various land formations of the world, and it will greatly help when studying a particular habitat or when traveling from one region to another. It does help to have read something about ecology and natural history so that you have a general idea about plant communities, geology, weather influences, animal habitats, and so forth when you visit a particular region. As naturalist/artists, we are viewing a habitat as a whole organism, even if we are studying its individual parts. (Refer to the Bibliography for some suggested readings on general natural history.)

When you go into the country to sketch, you are going for numerous reasons, some conscious and some not. You are going to sketch because it gives you an excuse to be where you want to be. You are going because you want to know what is out there. And, you are going because there is in us all that desire to make some form of record of a personal encounter with nature. Henry David Thoreau wrote in his journal on May 6, 1854, "It matters not where or how far you travel—the farther commonly the worse—but how much alive you are."

SKETCHING IN PARTICULAR HABITATS

Use the sections in this chapter as aids and the chart in Figure 3.27 as reference when going to the particular environments described. Whether you are alone, with a group of friends, or with a school or research group, it is always best to take some time to think out what you want to draw, how you wish to draw it, what tools you will use, and, most important, why you wish to draw it. Whether it be a landscape, plant, or animal, there is a broad range of both artistic and scientific methods for studying the countryside that can be

Figure 6.1
GUNNAR BRUSEWITZ (Swedish artist/naturalist)
Lillgardsbacken, March 29, 1978.
Pencil sketch with watercolor wash.

employed and have been employed for centuries. Choose which method (or methods) sems best for you.

Grasslands and Meadows

At one point, 42 percent of the world's land was covered by grasslands. Today, much of that is developed or cultivated. All grasslands commonly share a rolling-to-flat terrain, an animal life dominated by grazing and burrowing species, extreme contrasts in rains and drought, and plants and grasses. All are on successional stages, if left unmowed or unburned back to forest conditions. In this country, the largest grasslands, called *prairies* after the French word for grasslands, are now few and far between, and many of them have become refuges and park lands. It is rewarding to study grasslands and meadows for their diversity of small mammals, birds, insects, and reptiles, in addition to the grasses and other herbaceous plants found there. And to re-create on paper the open landscape, where sky meets grass and wind is ever present, is an exhilarating challenge for any artist.

Figure 6.2
CLARE WALKER LESLIE
Field sketch page done on the McKnight Prairie, Nothfeld, Minnesota, 1983. Technical drawing pencil.
The wind was blowing the pages of my journal and the sun was in my eyes. The biologist with me was giving out information so rapidly that I barely looked at the page as I raced to get it all down. Later, I was able to refine my notes. Having been so engrossed in absorbing the essence of this particular environment, its vision remains deep in my memory.

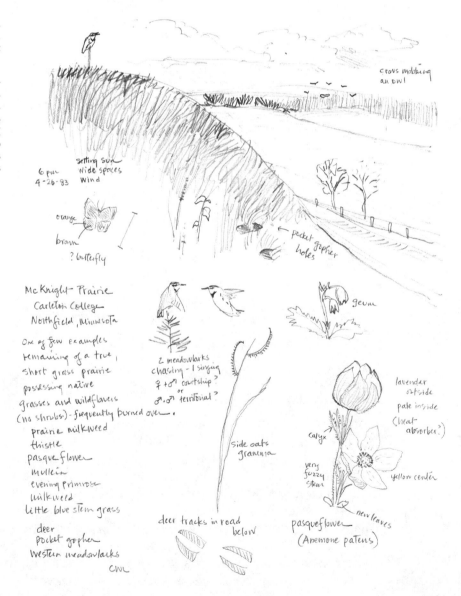

Driving out of Northfield, Minnesota
4.26.83
Sunny, 70°'s
5 pm
Rte 19

Corn
Soy
Pigs
grackles

400 mil. years old
Geologically -
limestone beds

Incredible sense of
physical space —

Figure 6.3
Three of a series of brief sketches done while driving in a jouncing pick-up
truck. Having the opportunity to draw this freely without concern for results,
enabled me to focus clearly on the Minnesota landscape and its essential
qualities, with barely a glimpse at the paper. To someone from the East Coast,
the open spaces of this region are truly magnificent. Here, I used a combination
of gesture and contour techniques.

Deserts, Canyons, and Arid Lands

Although the desert land in this country is small in contrast to the world's deserts, what we have is impressive and beautiful. Dry lands may receive as much rain as other regions, but it evaporates too quickly to be absorbed by the earth. As a result, all living things must adapt to extremes of heat, lack of water, and glaring sun. The best time to see any activity is at night, particularly around water holes. Spring is also a lovely time to visit the desert; this is when wildflowers take over the dry land and turn it into bursts of flaming colors. In the desert, plants have evolved to reproduce quickly while moisture is sufficient, resulting in the well-known sudden phenomenon called blooming of the desert. Also well known are the cacti and other exotic scrubby bushes that have evolved to survive the dry land existence. Go into the desert with awe and wonder and you will not leave disappointed.

Plate 1
JOHN BUSBY (contemporary British artist)
Watercolor field sketch of various gulls,
oystercatchers, a tern, and a shorebird.
Note that the artist has described the birds
in their natural position without attempting to
rearrange for a portrait likeness.

Plate 2
ERIC ENNION (20th century British artist)
Watercolor study of two tawny owls. Always the
naturalist, Ennion wanted to show the two
color phases of the owls—red-brown and gray.
These owls were painted from memory
after the pair was seen in a nearby wood.
Reproduced from The Living Birds of Eric Ennion *by*
John Busby (Victor Gollancz Ltd., 1982) p. 160. Courtesy of
the family of Eric Ennion.

Plate 3 (top)
JOHN BUSBY (contemporary British artist)
Landscape study (Mid Yel Voe, Shetland). Out in the
field, John may do three or four landscape
studies during his time outdoors. Once back in the
studio, he will rework a sketch a number of
times, changing composition and color relationships until
a final piece emerges. This outdoor sketch was done
with a charcoal-type pencil and a watercolor wash. It
displays the artist's concern with the simplicity
of expressing a landscape's impression.

Plate 4 (center)
CLARE WALKER LESLIE
Landscape study in felt-tipped pen and colored pencil.

Plate 5 (below)
GUNNAR BRUSEWITZ (contemporary Swedish
artist/naturalist)
Field sketch of a moose in northern Sweden.
Brusewitz will redo a field sketch, working it into a
finished piece by adding color once he is back indoors.
Then he will reproduce the piece into multiple
prints or cards, or as a plate for one of the many books
he has written on the natural history of Sweden.

Plates 6 and 7
JULIE ZICKEFOOSE (artist/naturalist from Connecticut)
Part of a series of studies of a great horned owl.
The model for the watercolor study above was a live bird
in a rehabilitation center for injured birds in
Connecticut. At right is a life study in pencil and
watercolor of a great horned owl.

Plate 8
CHARLES TUNNICLIFFE (20th century British artist)
Field study in pencil and colored chalk of a gray
lag goose. Tunnicliffe's notes say "in wing moult,
Y Felin (Wales), July 12, 1952."
Reproduced from A Sketchbook of Birds *by C.F. Tunnicliffe (New York:
Holt, Rinehart and Winston, 1979) p. 63. Permission to
reproduce given by the estate of C.F. Tunnicliffe and the
Midland Bank, Bangor, Wales.*

Plate 9
MICHAEL DI GEORGIO (wildlife artist from New York)
Watercolor study of a painted turtle.

Plate 10
CLARE WALKER LESLIE
Field sketch of an iris in a city garden. This sketch
was drawn in about thirty minutes with technical
drawing pen and colored pencil. Nothing was added later.

Monument Valley,
Utah – Arizona
Monday, 28th July, 1980.
Midday, brilliant sunshine.

The orange-red mesas, buttes and spires of Monument Valley
viewed from just south of Mexican Hat, Utah on route 163 (above).
Many of these sandstone monoliths tower as much as 1000 ft
above the valley floor, which is covered by clumpy desert shrubs
and occasional stunted trees. Navajo nomads first entered the
area perhaps in the 1600's, the original occupants having
abandoned the valley in the 1300's. Since then the Navajo
people have herded their sheep and other livestock and
raised small quantities of crops in this hot and arid environment.

West Mitten Butte and East Mitten Butte,
Monument Valley Navajo Tribal Park.

Figure 6.4 A & B
STEVE LINDELL
Two journal pages done with a felt-tipped pen in an 8½″ x 11″ hardbound
sketchbook. Steve kept a field journal while he drove across the United States
for the first time (See Figure 6.4B on next page.)

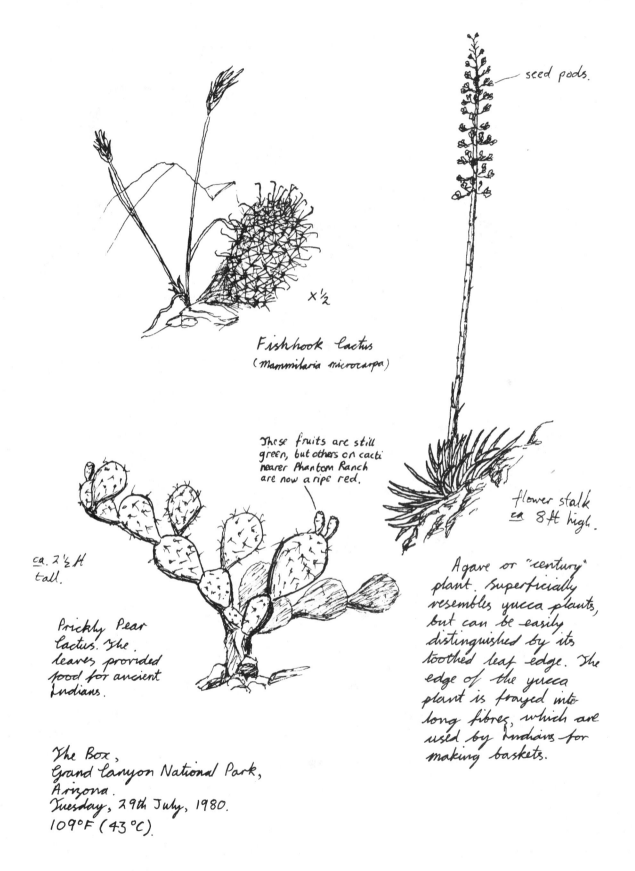

seed pods.

Fishhook Cactus
(Mammilaria microcarpa)

X ½

These fruits are still green, but others on cacti nearer Phantom Ranch are now a ripe red.

ca. 2½ ft tall.

flower stalk ca 8ft high.

Prickly Pear Cactus. The leaves provided food for ancient Indians.

Agave or "century" plant. Superficially resembles yucca plants, but can be easily distinguished by its toothed leaf edge. The edge of the yucca plant is frayed into long fibres, which are used by Indians for making baskets.

The Box,
Grand Canyon National Park,
Arizona.
Tuesday, 29th July, 1980.
109°F (43°C).

Farms and Farmlands

Farming has now taken over much of the open land that the pioneers once saw reaching far across this country. Whether it is on the vast grazing lands of the West or on the rock-strewn pastures of the Northeast, animals are keeping the land from reverting back into forest. Here are the places to sketch sheep, cattle, horses, and goats, as well as the barnyard chickens, pigs, ducks, and ever-present swallows and sparrows. Take a day to visit a local farm, sketching its landscape, the plants of the meadows nearby, and its various animals. It is a great way to see how a community of animals live together, as well as the operations of a farm.

Figure 6.5
WILLIAM H. WALKER (twentieth century American political cartoonist) Page from an 8½″ x 5½″ sketchbook. If a subject interested him, Walker would jot it down wherever he could find the space on the page. Study the ease with which he applied lines, attaining much color range in his drawings.

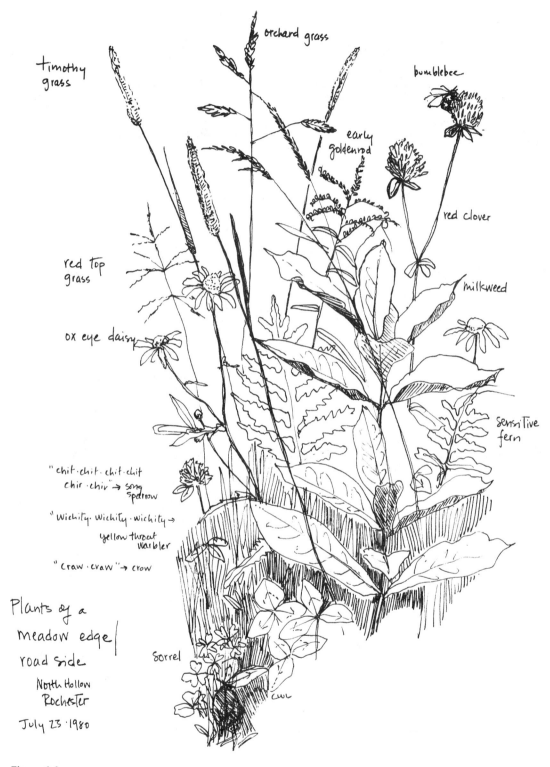

timothy grass

orchard grass

bumblebee

early goldenrod

red clover

red top grass

milkweed

ox eye daisy

sensitive fern

"chit·chit·chit·chit chir·chir" → song sparrow

"wichity·wichity·wichity → yellow throat warbler"

"craw·craw" → crow

Plants of a meadow edge/ road side

sorrel

North Hollow Rochester

July 23·1980

clul

Figure 6.6
Studies can be made of small habitats as a way of seeing what can be found within a defined area. Later, comparisons can be made with species found in other habitats or during another season. This felt-tipped pen sketch was recorded in an 8½″ x 11″ sketchbook while on a bicycle ride along a country road.

Sketching at Jensen's farm   Aug. 19   60°'s - windy but sunny
12:45pm.

I stirred up about 30 parent and
young barn swallows

Figure 6.7
Sketching can simply be the reason for getting outdoors on a nice day.

Figure 6.8
Sketches of horses in a local pasture.
Notice how I am mostly concerned with
gesture, not caring about detail or
accuracy of proportion. As the animal
moved, I would go on to another pose.
Just a few repeated lines were enough to
indicate a bit of volume.

Figure 6.9
Cows are harder to draw than one might think. It takes pages of sketches to get one or two looking "cow-like." When people saw me sketching, no one bothered me, or my car pulled over to the side of the road. If people see you with a sketch pad, often they will smile and leave you to your work. If I had simply been standing there staring, I might have caused more comment.

Figure 6.10
Vermont landscape.

Figure 6.11
We all think we know what roosters look like until we try drawing them. Not until I drew this cock did I learn the correct features of the common Rhode Island Red.

Figure 6.12
WINSLOW HOMER (American painter, 1836-1910)
Study of Boy Milking, pencil with white gouache.
Courtesy of the Museum of Fine Arts, Boston.

This is an exquisite little piece, probably one of hundreds that Homer did. All great artists have books and files full of similar sketches, which may or may not get worked into later paintings.

River Valleys

Water flows through many of our land-scapes, often defining geologic contours and vegetative diveristy as it wanders. Spend a day along a grassy bank, learning which plants, animals, and specific land features might be found there. Nighttime is a wonderful time to be near water, when images are dulled and sounds and smells are magnified, the moon or stars glitter across the water, and things rustle in the bushes. If you do not have your sketch-book, as was my situation in Figure 6.14, look hard at the scene, engrave its image as well as its mood in your mind. When back home, draw what best symbolizes the expe-rience you just had. Do not attempt to re-create it exactly. What is more important is the poetic expression of the situation's impression on you.

Figure 6.13
CATHY JOHNSON (illustrator from Missouri)
Pencil Study.
Observe how Cathy is able to apply varied tones to the trees and grasses by using the side of a pencil. Also, notice how by using *vertical* strokes for shadows she imparts a limpid quality to the water. This drawing was probably done in the same location as Figure 3.13.

East Valley/Fishing River - Excelsior Springs, Missouri
park is dotted w/ tiny mushrooms today

cuz 9pm 3-7-83

march full moon on back marsh

Figure 6.14
Night is a good time to try a sketch, when details are dimmed and subtle tones
of grays and blacks take over. A more careful drawing can be done from
memory once back indoors.

Woodlands

There are so many different types of woodlands that to define a typical one is nearly
impossible. Some are largely deciduous and
tion. In the tropics, forests are dense, rich
in number of plant species, and often very
wet while in the far north, forests can be
sparse, low in species diversity, and generally quite dry. Most of us live near woods
that are a mixture of hardwoods and evergreens, habitats typically composed of various kinds of maples, oaks, birches, wal-
nuts, pines, spruces, and hemlocks. As you
go farther up a mountain slope, deciduous
trees and shrubs decrease and evergreen
trees of balsam and fir take over. At the
mountain top, where wind and water
activity may be fierce, trees hug low to the
rock formations and what herbaceous

plants or lichens are there cluster in communities across the ledges. These plants
have specialized characteristics that enable
them to survive such alpine/arctic conditions.

When you enter a woodland, you
should consider it as a self-contained ecosystem, defined by the woody and herbaceous plants, by the birds and animals,
and by the weather and geology of the
region. In the northeastern United States,
85 percent of the land is wooded, a percen-
tage that comes close to that which existed
when settlers first came to this country. At
the height of lumbering during the nineteenth century, 85 percent of the land was
open land. This gives you an idea of the
control we have on the topography of our
environment.

The challenge in sketching woodland scenes is in the complexity of subject. Trees overlap, shrubs tangle in and out, and, often, we are too much *within* the landscape to get any perspective on it. Whatever you do, do not even try to sketch it all. Be selective; spend some time just walking and looking and then remain very simple in your compositional arrangement of foreground, middleground, and background. (For more information on landscape sketching, refer to Chapter 2.) Keep your landscapes small (as in Figure 6.16A) and juxtapose them with drawings of flowers or twigs or any animal that you see within this habitat.

The illustrations in this section were chosen to give you some ideas of the various ways one can look at woodlands. Take a small sketch pad and go examine the wooded area nearest you. Come back able to describe its features to someone who has never been there, with a series of sketches of its plants, animals, and landscapes.

Figure 6.15
REMBRANDT VAN RIJN (17th century Dutch painter)
Clump of Trees with a Vista, etching and drypoint.
Courtesy of the Museum of Fine Arts, Boston.

Perhaps Rembrandt etched this directly onto the plate while outdoors, or perhaps he took it from an earlier sketch. Whatever, his interest seems to be in conveying the impression of a wooded area rather than in depicting anything more realistic. Notice how much sunlight and atmosphere there is in this little study. What strokes did he use to depict leaves, branches, and shadow patterns? Rembrandt was a master of landscape portrayal and is an important artist to study.

droplets of rain on birch twig

first just hike and look as awarely as possible –
absorb visual and sensory perceptions
get to know habitat components –
flora and fauna
stop for no more than 5 min. + record
observations typical of area and of season

background
middleground
foreground

Select subject having interesting elements and some sort of design and a leading FOCUS

poly pody fern lichens & moss glowing

hemlock
beech
gray birch
no bird sounds

a.

Agassiz Rock Manchester 4·8·83

hear fog horn nearbye on coast
foggy. wet and chilly

Agassiz Rock, Manchester 4·8·83

nestled beside small oaks + cherries,
on top of a granite rock face:

rock lichen

bearberry

some green grass

new pink flower buds

an emerald green star-type moss

black oak

b.

Figure 6.16 A & B
Series of demonstrations for students during a class in sketching particular habitats.

large birches

Mink on
stream edge

Figure 6.17
WAYNE TRIMM (professional artist from New York)
Pencil sketch.
Drawn in a field journal while hiking Whiteface Mountain
in 1976, this might one day go into a painting, according to
the artist.

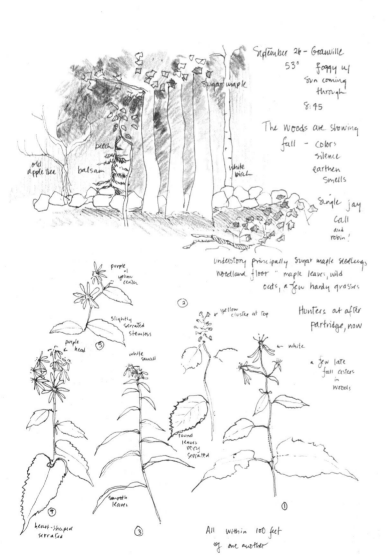

September 26 - Granville
53° foggy w/
sun coming
through
8:45

The woods are showing
fall - colors
silence
earthen
smells

Single jay
call
and
robin!

understory principally sugar maple seedlings
woodland floor " maple leaves, wild
oats, a few hardy grasses

Hunters out after
partridge, now

a few late
fall asters
in
woods

All within 100 feet
of one another

Figure 6.18
Field journal page drawn during a walk to examine a
particular woodland habitat near our house. Had I not
begun drawing asters, I would never have noticed there
were so many varieties along just one path. Colored pencil
was added for specific color notation.

Mountains

Mountains are fascinating, with their complex histories. In order to understand something of a mountain, we must know about geology and weather, and the history of time. The mountains we see today have undergone tremendous change in their 200 million years of existence. Therefore, when you go to sketch or draw a mountain, keep in mind the history you are looking at.

Since many of us do not have the opportunity to sketch mountains unless we are hiking in them or traveling past them, our chances of doing any lengthy drawing are probably limited. Whatever situation you are in, focus on the major shapes of your composition and leave out excessive detail. Spend no more than twenty minutes or you will begin to lose the spontaneity of your impression. Be sure to describe the sky and its clouds, if there are any, because setting a mountain in front of a further backdrop can help emphasize its height and majesty. Use the full tonal range of your pencil or pen to help give depth and contrast to your vista. Watch how the sun creates shadows and highlights along the configurations on the slopes. Drawing mountains is drawing mass and volume. This is your chance to really experiment with what you know about drawing techniques.

Figure 6.19
JEAN-BAPTISTE-CAMILLE COROT (French, 1796-1875)
A View of Mount Soracte from Civita Castellana, pen and iron-gall ink over graphite on white paper.
Courtesy of the Fogg Art Museum, Harvard University, Cambridge.

The achievement of this sketch is in the spontaneity of line and the simplicity of composition. Often the best sketches are those that are done without much forethought, as though from an unconscious source of inspiration. As in Figure 6.10, what has been left out has as much importance in terms of compositional strength as what has been put in. This study should be carefully analyzed for its compositional as well as expressive merits.

Figure 6.20
Drawn after a day hiking, while sitting on the porch of a Zealand Falls hut in New Hampshire's White Mountains. This composition has been very tightly designed to help control an otherwise overwhelming expanse of vista. The eye is specifically led through the various planes and out through the sky. Analyze how this has been done.

Figure 6.21
FRANCIS LEE JAQUES (American artist/naturalist, 1887-1969)
Pencil sketch of the Alps, 23½" x 32", 1935.

Reprinted by permission of the University of Minnesota Press *from Francis Lee Jaques*: Artist/Naturalist by Donald T. Luce and Laura M. Andrews (University of Minnesota Press, Publishers, 1982.)

To prepare for the large mural paintings that Jaques did for the American Museum of Natural History in New York, the artist had to spend an amount of time on field study expeditions. Often, conditions for painting outdoors were extremely difficult. Color photography had not yet been well developed. So, Jaques evolved a system of field sketching to effectively record essential information. His sketches emphasize color and principal contours, the results often having a paint-by-number effect. Once back in the museum, though, these sketches became the most accurate charts he would use to re-create the scene on a much larger scale. Francis Lee Jaques is one of America's greatest artist/naturalists. He believed that what could be seen and known about nature was endless and that as an artist he would do his best to bring this to the public's attention. He is perhaps best known for the impressive dioramas he painted for New York's natural history museum and for many scratchboard illustrations in books about his beloved northern Minnesota canoe country.

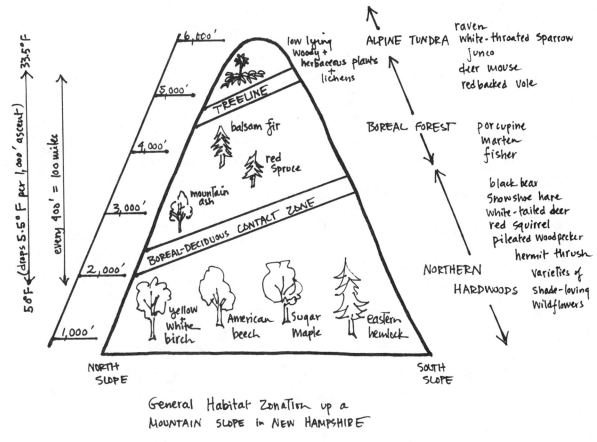

General Habitat Zonation up a
MOUNTAIN SLOPE in NEW HAMPSHIRE

Figure 6.22
When you are hiking up a mountain, consider the contrasts in zones as you
climb; watch the change in vegetation growth and animal activity along the
trail. This diagram can be changed to suit whatever mountains you are near.

SKETCHING WHILE BIRD WATCHING

Sketching birds in the field is a challenging experience even for the best of us. The bird does not pose for even a minute. Binoculars get in the way. The bird is but a speck in the distant marsh. You are too busy identifying it in the first place. Your pencil drops. And so on. But persevere, because the experience is well worth the struggle and will leave you with a much better idea of what you were seeing and what it was doing. Unless you have a camera with a high-powered lens, there is no other way than sketching if you want a visual record of the birds you have been watching and what they were doing.

First, practice by sketching birds at a feeder, in a pet store, or at a zoo. There, you can be relatively near your subject, perhaps be in a more comfortable position for drawing for a while, and have a good while to make many sketches of birds as they move about within close range. Another suggestion I give students (and I often follow myself) is to sketch birds from photographs and from field guides so that you can get the major identification features of the bird and have them on hand when you see it flash by outdoors (see Figure 2.14). Another preparatory place for sketching birds is in a science museum or biology department where there are mounted birds or stuffed specimens. Although the birds are not alive, you will have the opportunity to study coloration and feature details, and perhaps even handle the specimen without worrying that it will move.

Major outdoor habitats in which various species of birds may be found are:

- *City:*
  Pigeon, starling, house sparrow, chickadee, crow, purple finch
- *Suburbs:*
  Robin, blue jay, cardinal, downy woodpecker, junco

- *Country:*
  Song sparrow, meadow lark, kestrel, crow, mockingbird, red-tailed hawk
- *Woodlands:*
  Hermit thrush, great horned owl, nuthatch, various warblers, white-throated sparrow
- *Rocky coast in winter:*
  Common loon, common eider, various gulls, common goldeneye, bufflehead, white-winged scoter
- *Sandy beach in summer:*
  Various terns, yellowlegs, black-bellied plover, least sandpiper, song sparrow, common egret

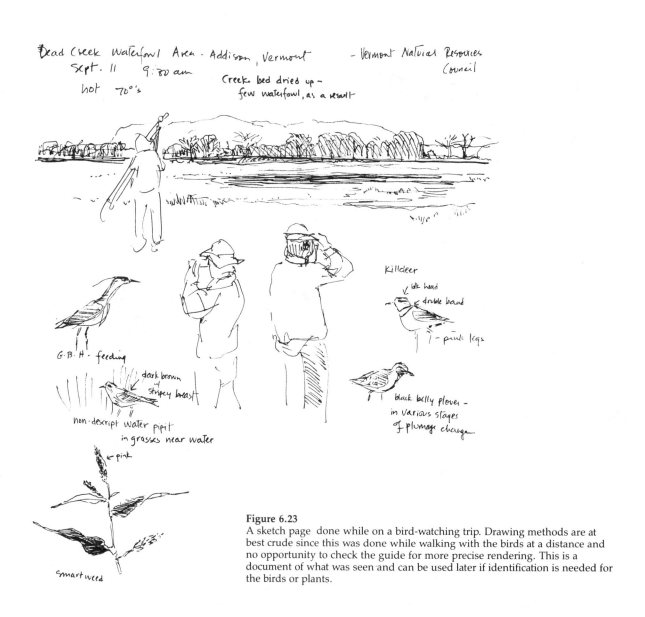

Figure 6.23
A sketch page done while on a bird-watching trip. Drawing methods are at best crude since this was done while walking with the birds at a distance and no opportunity to check the guide for more precise rendering. This is a document of what was seen and can be used later if identification is needed for the birds or plants.

Figure 6.24
WAYNE TRIMM (artist from New York)
Soft pencil field studies of a kestrel.

Figure 6.25
John Busby sketching nesting seabirds
(See Figure 7.24). I had the good fortune to
study with John at his home outside
Edinburgh. He would say, "Get down the
impression of the bird, in the most spontaneous and quickest way possible. What
you see in the field is not feather detail but
the bird alive and natural in its own
landscape. Draw that aliveness." The pen
he is using here is an ordinary, water
soluble felt-tipped pen to which he adds a
slight watercolor wash.

Figure 6.26

ERIC ENNION

Watercolor studies of several woodland birds.

This page, from his book *The British Bird*, has been reprinted here from *The Living Birds of Eric Ennion*, with commentary by John Busby (London: Victor Gollancz, 1982). Permission to reproduce granted by the family of Eric Ennion.

Eric advised his students to learn continually from the bird, "Whoever seeks to do so, must first train himself to observe and set down what he saw at once and quickly; and, secondly, should carry a bird's skeleton graven on his heart . . ." (p. 114)

Figure 6.27

LARRY MCQUEEN (ornithological artist from Oregon) Pencil sketch of a roadside hawk, drawn on a field expedition to Peru.

The artist said he did numerous gesture sketches of the hawk, which had flown into an exposed perch while he was waiting for other birds. With his telescope on a tripod, he was able to watch the bird and sketch at the same time.

When sketching birds outdoors, consider that they are always doing something and they are in that particular habitat for a *reason*. Do not just draw a portrait. Rather, have the bird in a behavioral posture that tells you something about it as well as about the habitat it is in. Above all, remember that in sketching birds outdoors, you are *not* drawing them, not yet. You are getting your eye to look at them better and are using the pencil (or pen) to help you. If necessary, draw from memory after the bird has flown off, as was done in Figure 6.23. Or, do a very diagnostic sketch if feature description is what you want. Keep your sketches small and simple. To draw birds well requires much looking and many pages of rough, crude, and partial scribbles before the likeness that you wish for will begin to form. All good bird artists have

Figure 6.28
Sketching while traveling in the car can be more rewarding than you might at first think. Each study can be a combination of numerous views, allowing you to choose what appears most typical of the area in which you are traveling. This type of sketching forces you to be extremely quick in your observation and keen in your memory abilities. It is good training for any form of field sketching. Try to capture essence and not detail.

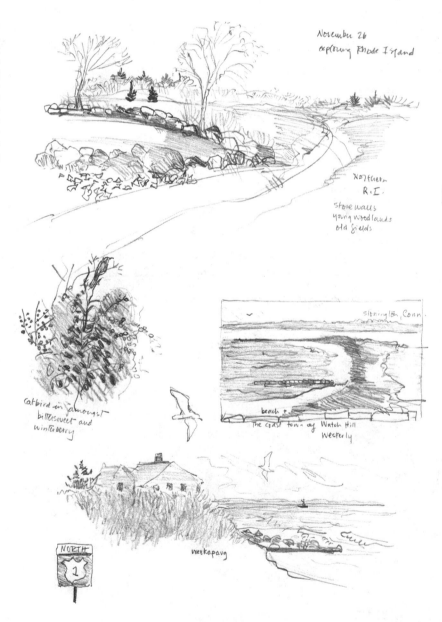

had years of experience. What they don't show you is all the drawings they threw out! Refer also to the section in Chapter 2 on sketching birds and also Chapter 7 (Figures 7.16 through 7.18, and Figures 7.24 through 7.29).

SKETCHING WHILE TRAVELING

Sketching while you travel, be it by car, bus, train, or plane, provides great oppor-tunity to observe with some detail a place you are passing through. Although your sketches will be very rough at times, this is a way of helping you notice tree shapes, varieties of roadside vegetation, changes from open field to woodland, species of passing birds, and so on as you travel from one region to another. In addition, this can be a great way of occupying time when you cannot do much else. It can involve your fellow passengers as they begin noticing characteristic features you should record. It can even develop into a treasure hunt or another sort of game if children are along.

Figure 6.29
I have learned much tree identifica-tion while driving. Comparisons between trees can be done along a highway where silhouettes stand out and wide variety among species often exists. Keep sketches small and attempt to convey the essential nature, or the principal gestalt, of a tree. Dusk is a good time to draw trees, when their silhouettes are clearly revealed.

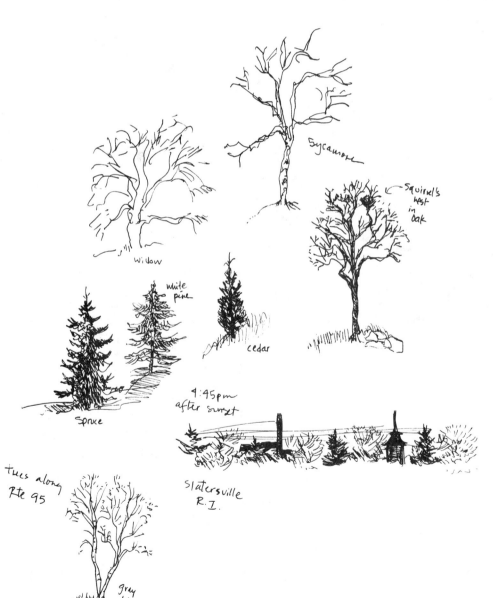

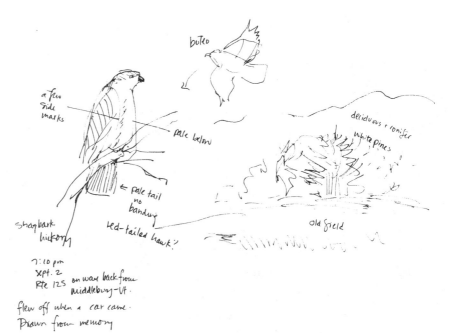

Figure 6.30
Quick notation of a hawk spotted while
driving. When I pulled over to the side
of the road to sketch, the bird flew off.
This is what I remembered.

Figure 6.31
WILLIAM DRURY (biology professor, College of the Atlantic)
The drawing was done in 1938 on a bicycle trip along the East Coast of the
island of Skye, while on vacation from school. Drury considers his sketchbooks
"my equivalent of a journal of travels."

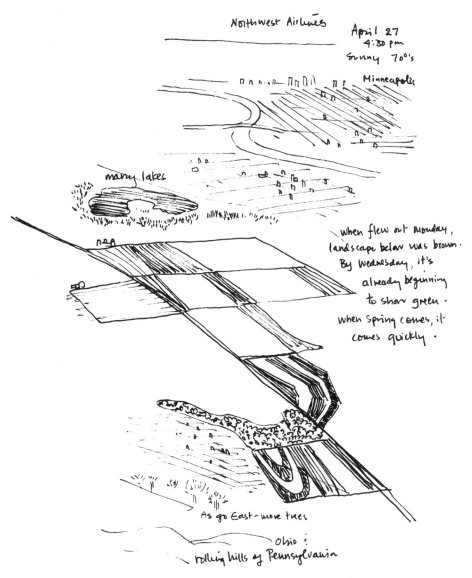

Figure 6.32
Drawing can even be done from a plane window. While sketching I took more careful notice of the beautiful designs in the plowed fields below. On the flight out, having *not* sketched I found I remembered little of the topography. By sketching on return, I became focused on how varied the landscape was as we flew east.

SKETCHING WHILE ON VACATION

Some people like to take cameras with them when they go on vacation. Others like to take their drawing pads. Still others like to take both. Try to set aside some time to draw each day while you are away. In pencil or in color, in a journal or in a sketch-book, wherever you are and however you do it, try to choose something to draw that will be characteristic of where you are and will be valued on return as a memento of your experience.

You can sketch while you are hiking, biking, walking, or sailing. You can sketch while waiting for others, early in the morning before anyone else is up or as a memory review just before going to bed. Specimens can be collected and sketched during a quiet time of day. Since it is really up to you what you wish to remember and how you wish to remember it, the "regulations" for drawing while on vacation are very loose. Let your writing flow easily into your drawings but do not let the writing dominate.

Journal sketching is a good way of drawing on vacation, since it helps give focus to your trip and helps you select the key features of the experience. (It is also an inexpensive way to keep an account of what you saw and did.) I have two friends who took their children, aged seven and nine, hiking for half a year in Nepal. The children made up for lost school time by keeping both written and sketched journals. Undoubtedly, those journals will long be treasured reminders of a rather unusual expedition.

Figure 6.33
CLARE WALKER LESLIE
Page sketched in front of a hotel in Cancun, Mexico.

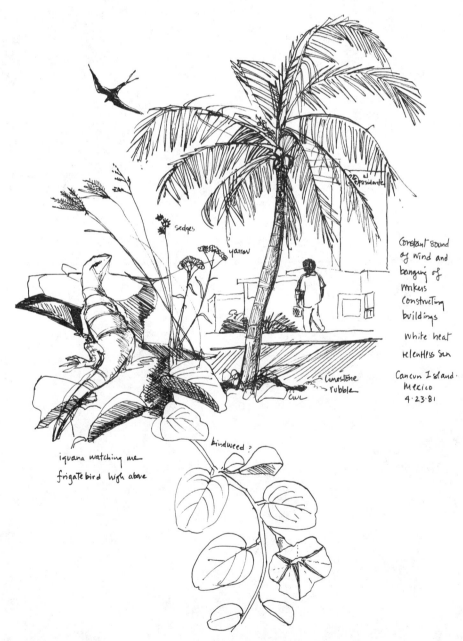

Figure 6.34
GUNNAR BRUSEWITZ (Swedish artist/naturalist)
Watercolor sketch done in Queensland, Australia.
When traveling, landscape studies should be kept small
and uncomplicated. It is important to record place, date
and time, and weather as much as possible.

Figure 6.35
WAYNE TRIMM (professional artist from New York)
Pencil studies of a Kodiak bear drawn while on an
expedition to Kodiak Island, Alaska in 1978.

Mid Yell
Shetland.
23 Aug 83

Dear Clare,

There are no post card views on sale here - so a short note instead . Hugh Miles and I are staying in a 'Motel' - actually a collection of portakabins out on a desolate peat moor, but overlooking a sea inlet, called here, a Voe.

The view is something like this :—

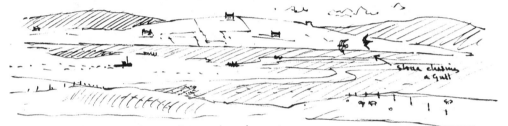

stoat chasing a gull

On the Voe, the pattern of water is always changing - reflecting skies, mirroring the hill and houses opposite or, swept by the wind and streaked by channels of different colours.

One sees many Shuas, Whimbrel, Ravens, Herons and Red-throated Divers, seals, Porpoises, and occasionally an Otter.

Despite some icy cold and wet "Winter" weather, we have been lucky in seeing Otters every day. Once one came ashore exactly in front of where we were crouching, and the other day a female, hotly pursued by a male, ran past me so close that I could have tripped them up by sticking out a foot. And they never saw me! Tonight at dusk one ran across the ground I was drawing 10 yards away. Unplanned encounters are the best!

When they come ashore the outer layer of fur opens in long streaky marbles.

Lovely appealing animals with an expression of benign good will.

Figure 6.36
Little descriptive studies can greatly enhance letters when one is traveling. The one shown here was written by John Busby on a trip to the Shetlands to draw otters for an upcoming book he was illustrating at the time.

Chapter 7
Sketching by the Water

Water can be sketched in many forms. Whether you live near a lake, pond, stream, river, or sea coast, each environment has its own distinct features and presents its own specific challenges for the sketcher. But water can be one of the more intriguing subjects to draw; it is always changing in form, always shifting its colors and moods, and always going somewhere.

It is important to take some time to observe water, studying its patterns and motions, watching the play of light and shadow across its surface, or just looking at it to try to understand its characteristics, both scientific and artistic.

The major challenges of drawing water are in making its surface appear flat (if it is), convincingly setting it into a given space, suggesting its liquid and limpid qualities, and re-creating the patterns of movement, light, and color along its surfaces. There are a number of techniques that, once learned, can make it much easier to draw water. By

studying the illustrations in this chapter, you will see how varied the methods can be. But before going on to the specific habitats, let me list a few suggestions you might try when drawing any form of water.

- Be sure to draw the *shape* of the water body carefully and have it angled correctly toward the line of the horizon. (Ask yourself: Is it a 20° or a 30° angle where the line of the water's edge meets the horizon? In woodland settings, the horizon must be sensed, since it usually is not apparent.) In Figure 7.1, the shape of the water body is a large triangle whose tip forms the central focus for the drawing.
- Be sure that all *major* lines describing the water's surface are horizontal. Any reflections or shadows can be vertical strips to suggest the water's reflective qualities. (Be sure to look at Figure 6.13.)
- Take care to bring banks *down* to the water's edge, describe reflections of adjacent trees and grasses, and generally con-

nect water to land. (Look at Figures 7.2 and Figure 7.3.)

- When drawing waves and ripples, pay close attention to the direction and flow of the water. Give emphasis to movement by actually drawing in directional lines (as in Figure 7.5) or by using contrasts in tone (as in Figure 7.10).
- Try different media and see how each describes water, whether it be pen or pencil, ink wash or colored pencil, watercolor wash or crayon.
- Try to convey the personality of the water if it is crashing against a rocky coast, rolling onto a sandy beach, or flowing quietly through a bit of woodland. This can be done in styles that range from very abstract to very realistic in conception.

Look at Figure 7.1 to see how these ideas apply.

FRESH-WATER LAKES, PONDS, AND MARSHES

Leonardo da Vinci once wrote that "water is the driver of nature." Without water, there would be no weather, no rain or snow, no flow into rivers and into seas. In fact, without water, much of the world would become too dry, too hot, or too cold to support life. Surprisingly, only five-thousandth of this water is fresh. The rest is salt.

Each body of water defines and is defined by its own particular habitat. When sketching, become familiar with the plants and animals that live within its depths and along its banks. What lives beside a northern bog will differ from what lives beside a southern lake. Geology and temperature have a lot to do with the formation of a water body and the life surrounding it. In

Figure 7.1
WILLIAM H. WALKER (American artist, 1871-1938)
La Salle, New York, August 18, 1892. A page from a sketchbook.

Watten
Reservoir
looking North
4-10-83

Figure 7.2
Sketched rapidly, this was done while standing on a hill over the reservoir.
Notice how flat the water's surface appears. This has been achieved by careful
attention to the shape of the reservoir, as well as to laying continuous lines that
are flat across the water surface. The shape of the reservoir is broad not narrow.
To help set the reservoir into a plane that has depth, the foliage in the
foreground is more distinct and darker to make contrast with the less distinct
and lighter background.

addition, conditions are never stable as
lakes become marshes, ponds become
bogs, and streams dry up. Therefore, when
sketching a fresh-water habitat, keep its
history in mind.

WOODLAND STREAMS
AND WATERFALLS

The shape and mood of a woodland stream
is largely defined by the land through
which it passes. Therefore, when sketching
a stream, it is important to consider the
types of trees, rocks, plants, and animals
that surround the passing water. The trees
may create reflections. The rocks may chan-

nel the path of the stream. The plants will
define the adjoining banks, and the animals
will provide clues to the location of the
water as well as to its quality.

If you are hiking beside a stream, stop
for a while. Sit on a rock and just watch
what is happening around you. Take in the
colors, sounds, and sights. Then, with an
easy pencil line, draw in a sketch that will
serve to remind you of this moment of quiet
observation. Look at Figures 7.3 and 7.4 for
ideas.

If the water is moving quickly over the
rocks or is cascading down over some rocky
falls, spend some time experimenting with
ways to draw spray, dropping water, and
swirling dark pools. See Figure 7.5 for suggestions.

Figure 7.3
DEBORAH PRINCE (illustrator from Massachusetts)
Study of Crum Creek, Pennsylvania, technical drawing pen.
Study how the artist has made the adjacent banks and trees dark to bring out
the light qualities of the creek. Broad at the base and narrow at the top, by
careful designing the creek flows into a deeply set background. Notice also
how, by use of both vertical shapes and horizontal strokes, the artist makes the
reflections on the surface give the water a flat as well as liquid appearance.

Stream flowing down Tuckerman Ravine

Figure 7.4
Field journal page by a student, done with felt-tipped pen and colored pencil. Notice how she has given an impression of the stream's movement by drawing lines along the flow of the water. The composition has been kept simple by concentrating principally on the path of the stream.

Figure 7.5
Demonstration done for a field sketching class with suggestions for drawing falling water over rocks.

1. First sketch the major compositional design. Make it flow as the water does.

2. Draw lines in the water to indicate surface planes as well as water texture.

3. Contrast tones to contrast planes (vertical + horizontal.)

4. Vary line strokes to show movement of water.

5. keep rock + foliage detail Minimal

6. Spend no more than 20 min. or Too Much detail will be put in

SANDY BEACHES, DUNES, AND SALT MARSHES

"The great rhythms of nature, today so dully disregarded, wounded even, have here their spacious and primeval liberty; cloud and shadow of cloud, wind and tide, tremor of night and day. Journeying birds alight here and fly away again all unseen, schools of great fish move beneath the waves, the surf flings its spray against the sun."*

Most of us have, at one time or another, been on a beach. We have walked through its open spaces. We have been blown by its winds and baked by its sun. And we have watched in fascination the eternal merging of water with land. But we have never tired of its scenery. The coast, where sea meets continent, will constantly be a source of inspiration and love for poets, musicians, artists, and for those of us who have been within its realm.

Ecology of the Sandy Beach, Dunes, and Salt Marsh

Since continual exposure to water and heat are primary concerns in a coastal environment, all animals and plants have adjusted to use such a specifically defined habitat to their best ability. During low tide, for example, many small fish and crustaceans burrow into the sands or mud. At high tide, they are active and feeding. At night, as the heat lifts, the beach may come alive with ghost crabs and minute beach hoppers. Since beaches are also seasonal in their ecology, and the presence of the plants and animals varies from summer to winter, it is best to know a beach at more than one time of year. Also, the various zones across a beach will determine what species may be

* Henry Beston, *The Outermost House* (New York: Viking Press, Inc., 1982), p. 2.

found and where. As shown in Figure 7.6, the foreshore beach has its own defined ecosystem that is different from the back salt marsh. You will not see great blue herons on a sandy beach because they do not feed on the organisms found there. Nor will you see dune grasses growing in a marsh because they thrive in arid sands.

The coast is at once a fragile zone and an eternal one. Sands are continually shifting, and seasons dramatically change a beach's image. Human development has channeled, bulwarked, and destroyed miles of our coastlines. Yet still the tides come and go, birds fly north and south over the shores, and the ancient horseshoe crabs come each spring to spawn on the sandy beaches. If we are to be true artist/naturalists, when we next go to the beach we will obey the "no trespassing, terns nesting" signs and keep our beach blankets off the struggling dune grasses. Perhaps our small sketches of the beach and its inhabitants might fall into the hands of those who will join with us in preserving what coastal landscapes still remain untouched.

When you go to the beach to sketch, take along a field guide to birds (particularly to shore and saltwater birds) and a field guide to plants (particularly of a beach environment). Take along also a satchel to keep your drawing equipment from getting wet or sandy. Be *sure* to take along a hat or dark glasses because the glare from the sun on your paper can make drawing difficult. Do twenty-minute sketches of various environments, not spending more time on any until you find one zone that particularly interests you; sketch the plants and various animals you find there and do a 3" × 5" landscape characterizing the view from that zone. Study carefully the sketches included in this section, and, if you are interested, read the books listed in the Bibliography by Henry Beston, Rachel Carson, John Hay, or others who wrote about sandy beaches.

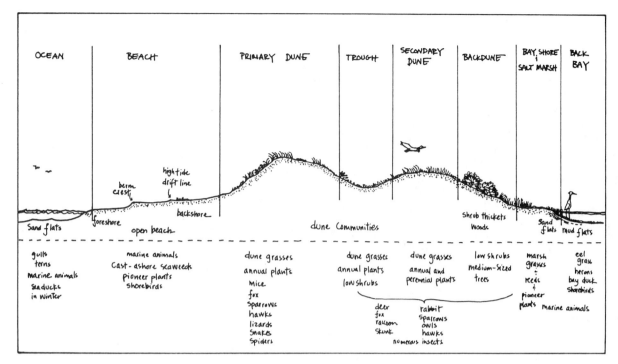

Figure 7.6
CLARE WALKER LESLIE
Diagram in technical drawing pen showing the cross-section of a typical barrier beach with ocean and beach on one side, and bay and salt marsh on the other. From *At the Sea's Edge: An Introduction to Coastal Oceanography for the Amateur Naturalist* by William T. Fox and illustrated by Clare Walker Leslie (Prentice-Hall, Inc., Englewood Cliffs, N.J., 1983).
Reproduced courtesy of Prentice-Hall.

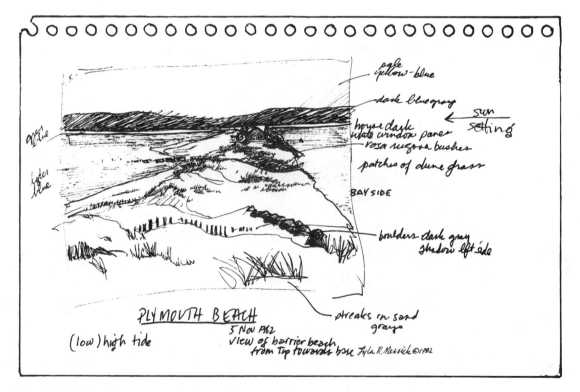

Figure 7.7
LYLA R. MESSICK (biological illustrator)
Sketchbook page of Plymouth Beach.
Lyla, who was interning at Manomet Bird Observatory in Massachusetts, used a felt-tipped pen for this sketch. She saw this scene as a potential painting, thus the notes on color.

Figure 7.8
WILLIAM H. WALKER (American artist, 1871-1938)
Sketchbook page by William H. Walker with a study for a potential painting. How has he designed the composition to achieve a sense of great distance? How has he described the sky in contrast with Figure 7.9? And how has he defined wave motion here and in Figure 7.9? Sketching within a frame was a common technique my grandfather used to help set the size of his sketch, as well as to give it a compositional binding. This sketch is only 3¼" x 6" and might have been done quickly before he went back to his family or further along the beach.

Figure 7.9
WILLIAM H. WALKER (American artist, 1871-1938)
Sketchbook page of Duxbury Bay, Massachusetts.
The artist loved to sail. This was one of many pages he did from a boat. Though appearing simple, this sketch has achieved a feeling for space, air, and light with but a few well-understood strokes.

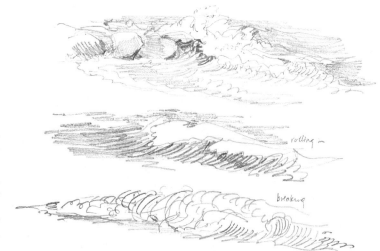

Figure 7.10
Studies of waves breaking onto the beach. Follow the direction of the waves' passage with your pencil, angling the strokes along the surface planes. Many studies such as these should be done if you are to draw waves with any success.
It also helps to draw waves and water from photographs where individual shapes can be analyzed more clearly.

Figure 7.11
WILLIAM H. WALKER (American artist, 1871-1938)
Sketchbook page of Duxbury Beach, Massachusetts, with color notes and layout ideas for a potential painting.
In those days, artists sharpened their pencils with a knife. They made edges on the sides of their leads, often keeping the ends blunt. Employing this method, they could get broad and narrow strokes within one line and achieve dark and light tones with just a little pressure of the hand. Notice how much tonal gradation there is in this sketch, as well as variation in line quality. Today, with our sharp-tipped and harder leads, we use the sides of our pencils less and often have fewer color ranges in our sketches. This was probably done with a 5B pencil.

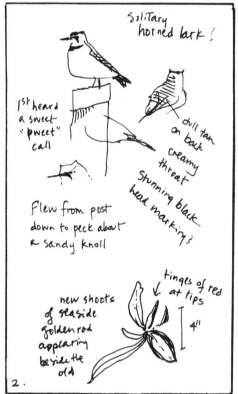

Figure 7.12
Some sixty years later, I was walking on the same beach my grandfather had once spent so many years enjoying. How different are the purposes for our sketches and our styles, yet we are both attempting to use drawing to know the beach better. I had gone to take a short walk before it rained. All I had with me was a 3" x 5" note pad and a felt-tipped pen both of which I had casually stuck in my pocket. Yet, in thirty minutes of walking, *because* I had these scraps of paper and so was prepared to record what I saw, I noticed an incredible amount. In fact, had I not bent down to draw the wormwood plant, I would not have noticed the horned lark on the post right beside me. The sketches aren't much but they are clear memory pieces of a rainy day on the beach, spent alone with the raw elements. This is a good example of how habitat sketching can be done with little equipment and minimal technique.

Figure 7.13
Sitting low beside a dune and out of the cold wind, I sketched before my hands froze. But I love this study as it captures the mood and simple poetry of a bleak November beach. (The pencil tones were added when back in the car.)

Figure 7.14
CLARE WALKER LESLIE
Field Sketch of Eastham, Massachusetts (1978)
Observe contrasts in vegetation and in the definition of receding land masses to attain a sense of distance and space. What methods were applied to give the marshes their flatness? When sketching landscapes outdoors, it is important to convey a certain mood of the place and a recognition of the specific season as well. It was a cold blustery autumn day then, with ducks restlessly moving about in preparation for their flights south.

Long Point, Duxbury
11·30·82
Only the sound of gulls calling and the wind in metal rigging

low tide

CWL

soft-shelled clam

ribbed mussel

blue mussel with rock barnacles

Atlantic razor clam

marsh grass

dogwhelk

periwinkle

crableg in amongst seed heads and grass bits — green crab?

gull feather

eel grass

sea lavender

fucus

boat shell

3·8·83 CWL Duxbury

gatherings from a bayside beach

Figure 7.15
The landscape was laid in outdoors and the objects were gathered in my pockets during a cold winter's walk along the tidal marshes. Back indoors, I could draw the collections at leisure. A felt-tipped pen was used with pencil for shading. This is another example of how pieces can be recorded when collected from a particular habitat. It makes for an interesting treasure hunt to go see what you can find in a specific location such as ocean beach, bayside beach, salt marsh, or dune.

Figure 7.16
CHARLES TUNNICLIFFE
(twentieth century British artist)
Studies of an Immature Herring Gull,
pencil and colored pencil.
From *A Sketchbook of Birds* by Charles Tunnicliffe,
introduction by Ian Niall (London: Victor Gollancz,
1979) p . 4.
Published by permission of the Tunnicliffe Estate.

Figure 7.17
R. RICHARD GAYTON (Illustrator from California)
Attitudes of Marbled Godwit, HB pencil.
In a letter describing his work, Richard said, "I
utilize a method in keeping my field sketchbook that
may be of interest to you. After returning from an
expedition, I will file the sketches in folders appropriate to the particular subject. There is a folder for
ungulates, and so on." (Personal communication,
January 1983.)

Figure 7.18
FRANK W. BENSON (nineteenth century American artist)
Pencil sketch of a canvas-back duck.
Courtesy of Mr. and Mrs. Donald Seamans.

Although Benson was best known as a portraitist, his love of duck hunting in
his native Massachusetts inspired him to do many sketches, as well as etchings
and paintings, of the birds he saw while out in the hunting boat. His ability to
describe the essence of a bird, without much detail or sometimes even
important accuracy of features, has brought Benson respect among many
patrons of bird art.

ROCKY COASTS

Although the topography of a rocky coast
seems to differ from region to region, there
are characteristics common to the rocky
coastlines of the world. All have a shape
that has its evolution in the roots of geologic history, all are harshly refined by sea
and weather, and all provide a challenging
environment for the plants and animals
that cling to their rocks. Scientists have
done zonation studies and found the plant
arrangement, or *algal zones* as they are
called, to be comparable on Norwegian and
Australian and North American coasts.
Similarly, the species of mollusks, crabs,
fish, and birds that inhabit these regions are
comparable. Therefore, whether you live
on the East or West Coast, in Europe or
America, the rocky coast you clamber along
will have relatives on other continents.

Figure 7.19
NANCY S. HART (scientific illustrator from Illinois)
Pebble Beach, Monhegan Island, Maine, July 1982,
A double sketchbook-page drawing done in drawing pen.
Notice the marvelous variety of line strokes used here to contrast the differing
zones on the shore edge—pebbly beach, rocks, branchy debris, grasses, and
woodland evergreens.

Figure 7.20
CLAIRE WALKER LESLIE
Diagram showing the zonation of life on a typical North Atlantic rocky shore.
From *At the Sea's Edge: An Introduction to Coastal Oceanography for the Amateur
Naturalist* by William T. Fox and illustrated by Clare Walker Leslie (Englewood
Cliffs, N.J.: Prentice-Hall, Inc., 1983).
Zonation on rocky shores comprises a series of bands of varying widths
defined by specific plants and animals that have adapted themselves to live
best within a given distance from the sea's waves.

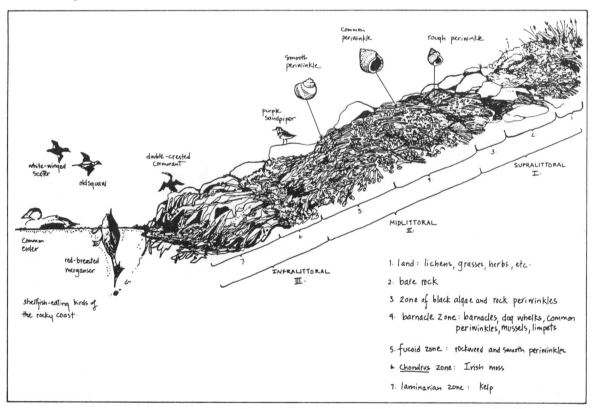

The Ecology of the Rocky Coast

The ecology of the rocky coast may at first seem less varied than that of the sandy beach because much of the life occupies areas on the rock faces, which, at certain times of day, are either fully or partially covered by water. In addition, during storms or during winter, many creatures disappear into crevices or lie dormant within deeper sea realms.

In order to sketch along the coast with any understanding of its natural history, it is a good idea to become familiar with what may be found there. Look at the diagram in Figure 7.20. Locate a field guide or two on the plants and animals of the rocky coast near you. Then with guide and sketch book in hand, set forth for a day of adventure with only the sounds of the surf and the crying gulls for company.

Figure 7.21
KATHRYN M. CONWAY (biological illustrator from New York)
Sketch page animals in a tide pool on the eastern coast of New Zealand's south Island, done with H technical drawing pencil on tracing paper.
"Upon graduation I received a fellowship to study independently overseas. My project focuses on the illustration of the flora and fauna of New Zealand, Japan, and other Asian countries. This sketch page was drawn in the lab. The animals were kept alive in circulating sea water, and removed for only a few minutes at a time for observation under the microscope. They were very difficult to draw, being in constant motion, retreating from the harsh microscope light. The opportunity to draw live sea invertebrates made me realize how very dead a pickled museum specimen appears! I am relying on these pencil sketches, notations and color photographs to complete a full-color painting of tidal pool life." (Personal communication, March 1983).

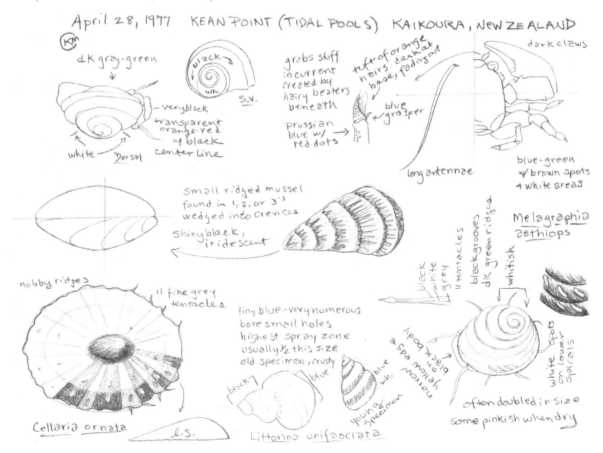

TIDAL POOLS

Northeastern Univ. Marine Biol. Lab.,
Nahant, Mass.
Sunday, 17th May, 1981.
2.00 - 3.30 pm.   ~65°F.

High Pools ⟹ Flooded only during highest tides and during storms. Heat (during summer) and inaccessibility keep grazing species scarce. Hence green algae is plentiful. Brown and red algae cannot exist this high.

Middle Pools ⟹ Flooded at every high tide. Rockweeds (Fucus and Ascophylum) are now common. Mussels, periwinkles and limpets are abundant. Green algae is still quite common, but will become more scarce later in season as grazer population increases. First barnacles appear. Some kelp.

X 2;
white.

Egg mass
of periwinkle
on kelp leaf.

X 1 ; olive green

Ascophylum.

Low Pools ⟹ Nearer low tide mark. Rockweeds still predominant algae, but kelp also now quite common, and some red algae are present. Sea urchins and crabs are common. Notice large numbers of small, easily removed, ca. two week old barnacles. Larger barnacles observed filtering pool water for food with delicate red foot.

Fucus

X 1
dark olive green

26

Figure 7.22
STEVE LINDELL (British chemist)
Sketchbook page of Massachusetts tidal pools drawn with a felt-tipped pen in an 8½" x 11" hardbound sketchbook.

153

Newport, Rhode Island
low 30°'s Sunny
Very windy
11-26-82   Cold!

bufflehead in a cove
below one of the many mansions

high seas
much white surf

cur

Cliff Walk: loons in winter plumage
           ← cricket chirping!
              a few roses still
              in bloom on the
              lawn of one mansion

Figure 7.23
Sketched from a car window when it was too cold and windy to draw
outdoors. Felt-tipped pen sketches were smeared with a wetted brush to add a
bit of tone. Having never been to this area before, sketching was a good way to
learn what typified the region.

Figure 7.24
JOHN BUSBY
Page of seabirds nesting on a rocky cliff overlooking the Firth of Forth, Scotland. Although this page was done in the studio, John used primarily his memory of the birds and some accumulated sketches to render a depiction of restless activity and the interchange among the birds in a sea bird colony. (John rarely draws birds from photographs, preferring the freshness of his field sketches and the keeness of his own memory.)

Puffins, Shags, Razorbills, Gulls and Gannets.

John Busby 82.
Craigleith Island Firth of Forth.
Bass Rock in the background.

Figure 7.25
Photograph of John Busby (second from left) sketching with British artist David Measures and his son.
David is sketching using watercolors held in a small box in his hand and washed on with a brush and his fingers. (His studies were loose, abstract impressions.) I was there with them on the Bass Rock, Firth of Forth, Scotland on a rainy, chilly day in June when the seabirds were at their peak of nesting. The air was thick with crying and circling gannets, kittiwakes, shags, and puffins. Sketching was wild and very exciting. There was so much commotion and drama, and our pages kept flapping in the wind and rain.

Figure 7.26
CHARLES TUNNICLIFFE
Pencil and colored pencil studies of guillemots From *A Sketchbook of Birds* by
Charles Tunnicliffe, introductions by Ian Niall (London: Victor Gollancz, 1979),
p. 23.
Published by permission of the Tunnicliffe Estate.

Although Tunnicliffe was a magnificent wildlife artist, he perhaps showed his
greatest skill in his sketches and studies.

Figure 7.27A
DR. WILLIAM H. DRURY (biology professor
at College of the Atlantic, Maine)
Studies of noddies in the South Pacific.
These are part of a sketchbook he kept while on a Navy ship during
World War II.

Figure 7.27B
DR. WILLIAM H. DRURY
Another sketchbook page drawn at the same time as Figure 7.26.
Observe how Dr. Drury has shaped the headlands by the direction
of his pencil.

TROPICAL SEAS AND ISLANDS

It is the lucky vacationer who gets to leave a northern winter for the sun and sand of a tropical island. If you have any room, take along your sketching gear. During those moments when it is too hot to do much else, a quiet time sketching shells or palmettoes or flapping pelicans can provide a means for remembering just what it was like when you tell your friends back home. Sketching can greatly enhance a trip as it is a tool for focusing on a specific environment that may be otherwise quite unfamil-

iar and quite overwhelming. It gives you an opportunity to see just how different or just how similar this environment is to the one that you have come from. And, sketching can be done alone or with others, and it does not cost a *peso* to do.

Try to do a sketch page a day, combining it with any diary you are keeping, with photographs or postcards, or with any research you may be doing. (Look at Figures 6.33, 7.22 and 7.28 for sketch page ideas.) However you use your sketching, make it a part of your daily life, and you will find the world of nature to be a fascinating and continually enjoyable companion.

Figure 7.28
CARLA BRENNAN (artist from Massachusetts)
Field sketchbook page of Mona Island, Puerto Rico, April 1980.
This sketch was drawn with a 2B Drawing pencil.

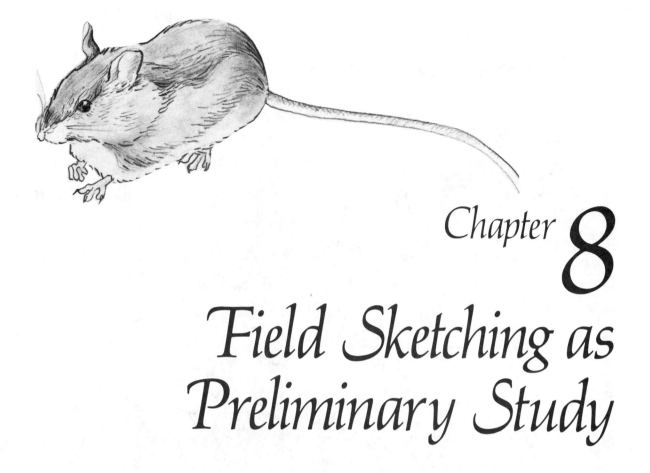

Chapter *8*

Field Sketching as Preliminary Study

The illustrations included in this chapter show the various ways that the artist uses field sketching in the preliminary stages of working up a finished piece of art, whether for artistic or scientific purposes. As mentioned in earlier chapters, artists use numerous methods and references when developing finished pieces. They will draw from photographs, from previous drawings and paintings, from skins and mounted specimens, and from the live animal or plant specimen itself. But virtually all artists derive their initial concept of a finished work from the early sketches, where the nascent forms are first examined.

Once more, to clarify terms, if a sketch has been done outdoors without a prearrangement of subject material, I use the word "field sketch." If a sketch has been done as part of working up a finished piece, or the subject material has been rearranged, I call this a "study sketch." A study sketch may be done indoors or outdoors. A field

sketch is mostly done outdoors. But remember, much of this is semantics and may change in definition from artist to artist. Most importantly, remember that sketches are done as processes in seeing and not necessarily as finished pieces.

In gathering examples of artwork for this chapter, I interviewed four artists whose works are quite different, and yet all clearly stated again and again how basic to their art is the time spent outdoors observing and sketching. Interspersed among the interviews are examples of studies done by other artists showing either the process from initial sketch to finished piece or simply the original sketches (as in Figures 8.6 and 8.11) if unable to get the final work.

Peg Estey is a freelance natural history artist based at Harvard's Museum of Comparative Zoology and is currently directing a certificate program in scientific and technical illustration at the Rhode Island School of Design/Continuing Education. When I

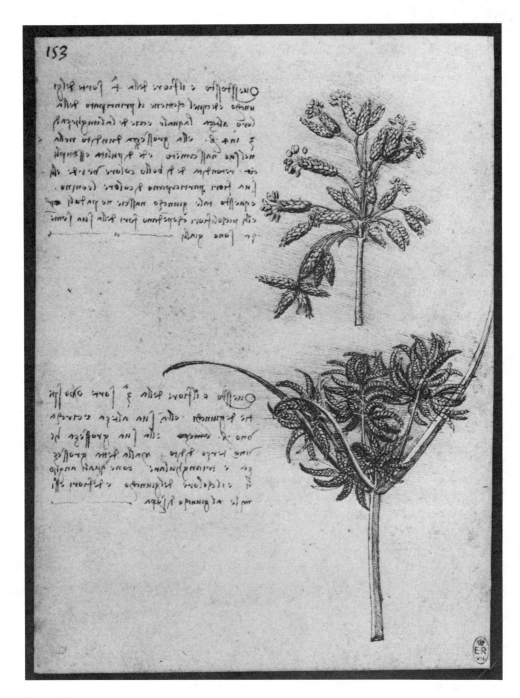

Figure 8.1
LEONARDO DA VINCI (Italian Renaissance painter)
Study sketches of rushes, drawn around 1513 from the Royal Library, Windsor Castle, England.
Permission to reproduce granted by Her Majesty the Queen.

Da Vinci was one of the first artists to look at nature as a subject for scientific study. He did hundreds of drawings and notes that he had hoped to establish into an encyclopedia of treatises on such topics as hydrodynamics, aerodynamics, the cause of earthquakes, fundamentals of engineering, and various plant studies. To keep his notes secret, he wrote them in a cryptic fashion. Today, art historians agree that it was Leonardo da Vinci who first created the modern concept of scientific illustration.

interviewed her, she had recently returned from a trip to the Galápagos Islands where she had led a group for Lindblad, an organization that takes groups to see world-wide places of natural interest. One of her goals had been to show people the methods and values of keeping simple journal/sketchbooks. She said that once over the initial fears and inhibition of drawing, participants became intrigued with how much they could record by sketching, more than by picture-taking. Figures 8.5A and B show one of Peg's many field sketches and then the finished drawing done on return for the Log of the cruise, sent by Lindblad to all participants.

Figure 8.2
OLAUS MURIE (twentieth century American naturalist)
Field sketches of coyote in pencil and watercolor wash.
Reproduced courtesy of the Grant Teton Natural History Association, Moose, Wyoming.

Murie used these field studies which he sketched in 1928, to help in illustrating his various scientific writings on North American mammals and birds. One book that he is perhaps best known for, *A Field Guide to Animal Tracks*, is in the Peterson Field Guide Series published by Houghton Mifflin. Dr. Allen W. Stokes, professor Emeritus of Utah State University said of Murie's work: "There is a lesson in these sketches. There is no magic formula for becoming a natualist; certainly not a college degree in biology. Instead one must be willing to spend patient hours in the field, constantly asking questions . . . Olaus painted, not with selling any of this work in mind, but strictly to further understanding of the animals he was observing."

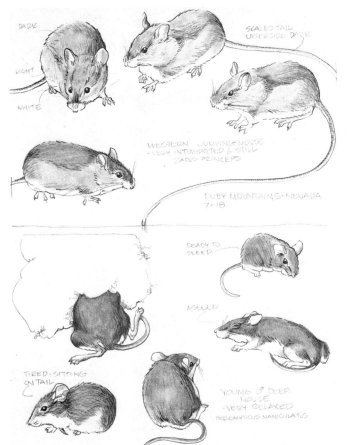

Figure 8.3
WAYNE TRIMM (wildlife artist from New York)
Life studies of a female short-tailed weasel and young (1956), drawn in pencil and watercolor.
Trimm used studies such as these when he did the color plates and pencil illustrations for *A Country-Lover's Guide to Wildlife* by Kenneth A. Chambers.

Figure 8.4
BETH D. MERRICK (biological illustrator from California)
Life studies of a western jumping mouse and a deer mouse in "Ebony" Eberhard/Faber #6325 pencil and smudged pencil tones.
Beth noted, "I sketch road kills and live traps on field trips and 'vacations' in order to compile reference material for future drawings as well as to increase my understanding. The mice sketches will be used this year in my Christmas serigraphs." (Personal communication, March 1983).

Figure 8.5A
PEG ESTEY (natural history artist from Massachusetts)
A field sketch in black ball-point pen of Galapagos marine iguanas, drawn on
site at Punta Espinosa, Fernandino, Galapagos.

Figure 8.5B
PEG ESTEY
Finished drawing of the same subject done with pen and Indian ink on plastic
vellum for the Lindblad Log of the cruise, a document of the trip sent
afterwards to all participants.

Peg had the following comments to make about the importance of field sketching in her work as an illustrator:

The act of field sketching allows me an experience when I can concentrate less on technique and more on observation—when I can simply get down on paper what I see. It is a direct contact with an object when nothing intervenes such as "is this a 'good' drawing," "will it sell," "am I using the right medium," etc.

For a biological illustrator, accuracy is essential as the work is often used for research purposes. Scientists require precise representations of their data, so there is no room for experimenting with form. When sketching in the field, on the other hand, I don't have to worry about the 'success' of the drawing because what will always be successful is the *experience* of seeing/drawing.

The best way to remember something is by drawing it. Anyone can draw what they are most familir with. In order to learn something better, to understand it better, direct observation and a quick sketch of its elements can teach more than three hours with an encyclopedia.

I do use photographs in my finished work for reference on feature details, posture, or habitat. But, it is my initial field sketch that I trust the most for the overall accuracy of gesture and form. I advise students to follow this sequence when using reference materials:

1. The actual, living specimen
2. *Your* drawings made from the living specimen
3. *Your* photographs made from the living specimen and much less useful,
4. Someone else's photographs
5. Taxidermy specimens and study skins
6. Someone else's drawings

One more advantage of working in the field is that you can be right there with the animals. The fresh air is great for the spirit!

Figure 8.6
JOHN BUSBY
Field studies of otters in the Shetland Islands, EE pencil and watercolor wash.
John spent a month up in the Shetland and Orkey Islands doing numerous studies such as these for a forthcoming book on otters by a British animal behaviorist. Back at home, he assimilates bits and pieces from all his sketches to work up the finished drawings.

Handwritten annotations on studies:
ears forward
ears look lazy –
eyelashes!
light source
ears back
(grass medium to
short, feet somewhat
hidden.)
J. Powzyk

Figure 8.7
JOYCE A. POWZYK (biological illustrator from New York)
Series of studies and the final drawing of a grey kangaroo
in Tooloom, Australia.
Materials used: "Various pencils, sketch pad sturdy enough for field work and
binoculars." Final drawing done with technical pen. Joyce traveled to Australia
to gather sketches and ideas for a children's book on Australian wildlife. To
educate children on the behavioral poses and activities of these animals it was
necessary to sketch predominantly in the field.

Julie Zickefoose graduated from Harvard University and is now employed as a freelance bird artist and field naturalist living in Connecticut. In an interview with her concerning her work (see Color Plates 6 and 7 as well as Figure 8.8) Julie had these comments to make:

> I divide my time between conservation work and art work, with inevitable overlap between both fields. Having been commissioned to illustrate *Birds of Insular New-foundland*, I spent part of the summer up in the countryside there, studying and making copious sketch/notes concerning the birds I must paint as well as their habitats. These sketches I will rely on heavily when I go to do the final, color plates back in my studio.
>
> Looking at a creature with the intent to draw it is, for me, entirely different from merely observing it. I may notice that a golden plover's head is small in proportion to its body, but when I sketch it, I must

Figure 8.8
JULIE ZICKEFOOSE (bird painter and field naturalist from Connecticut)
Field study in pencil of a male and female moose.
In commenting on her experience sketching the male moose seen at a local zoo, Julies noted, "Simply looking at that moose would never have acquainted me with just *how* different it was . . . By the time it got up and plodded off, I understood much more about how a moose is put together than I could have through any other references."

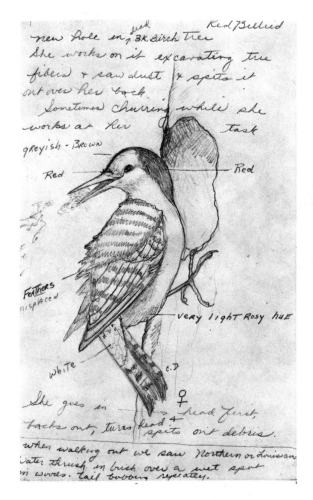

Figure 8.9
CAROL DECKER (wildlife artist from New Jersey)
Two sketch pages and a final painting
of two red-bellied woodpeckers.
Carol spent many days observing this pair while
they excavated a nest hole and eventually reared
two young. The lifelike description of these birds as
is evident in her painting could not have resulted
without this type of first-hand experience.

quantify. How small: How does it hold its head? How large are the eyes? Sketching is almost like making a series of minute measurements, all over an animal's body. It's made more challenging when your subject is alive and moving.

I've always field sketched. In my studio, I am at sea without my sketches. Their values are several:

First, a carefully drawn life study is an invaluable reference—the last word in accuracy. With color, another level of information is added. Accuracy—correctness of form, attitude and color—is my paramount concern in drawing and painting. Therefore, I feel comfortable drawing only organisms with which I've had the opportunity to become familiar with—in life. Once I've made sure I am correct in

my rendering, beauty and grace flow in. Most of my sketches are more pleasing to me than my finished paintings because they are the first, unselfconscious efforts to understand a creature.

Second, sketching is a quick way to begin the processes of learning to understand a previously unfamiliar form.

Third, sketching (and drawing) from living subjects is the best way I've found to battle off preconception. My greatest enemies in drawing are my assumptions about what an animal looks like or how it moves. I don't like to rely on photographs because they often can be misleading. But I do use them for reference. Drawing from my assumptions would be great if I illustrated fantasies, but it's not generally approved of by field guide publishers!

Figure 8.10
TASHA TUDOR
Pages from one of many sketchbooks kept by this well-known and much loved illustrator of childrens' books.
Permission to reproduce given by the artist.

Tasha Tudor draws what she sees around her immediate home; dogs intermingle with goats, and children with rabbits. What she sketches often goes into a colored illustration for one of her many cards or books.

Figure 8.11
TERRENCE SHORTT
Life studies of a peregrine falcon in watercolor wash (Fort Ross, Somerset Island, Northwest Territories, 1938).
Terrence Shortt is both an accomplished naturalist and artist. He did many studies such as these over the years while preparing the various dioramas, publications, and other illustration work for the Royal Ontario Museum. *The Complete Outdoorman's guide to Birds of Eastern North America* by John P. S. MacKenzie is one of many books in which Shortt's superb pen and ink and watercolor work can be seen.

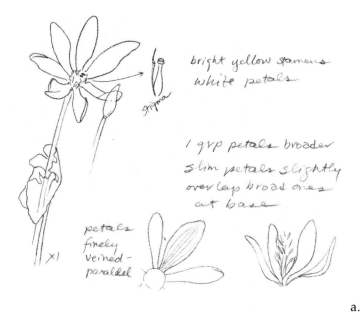

bright yellow stamens
white petals

1 grp petals broader
slim petals slightly
overlap broad ones
at base

petals
finely
veined -
parallel

a.

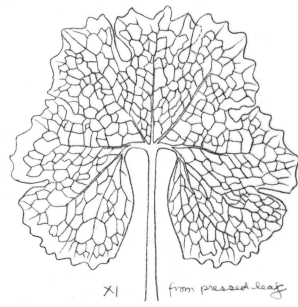

×1 from pressed leaf

b.

root bleeds
orange sap
when cut

light green
stems

papery
sheath

tough
roots
thick
rhizone

c.

Figure 8.12
KATHRYN M. CONWAY (biological illustrator from New York)
Steps toward the final scientific illustration of bloodroot,
Sanguinaria canadensis from R. S. Mitchell's contributions to a flora
of New York State V, *Berberidaceae* through *Fumariaceae*, New York
State Museum Bulletin 451 (1982).
Reproduced with permission of the Biological Survey, New York State Museum.

a   Specimen sketched on location (5 lead mechanical pencil).
b   Study from a pressed leaf, with others drawn from photographs.
c   One of several studies from parts of fresh specimens.
d   Final drawing, composed from the sketches and done on 3-ply
hot press Bristol board with flexible pen and ink. The
drawings show the whole plant in a natural position, and
include enlarged details of taxonomically important characteristics (i.e., seeds and flower parts).

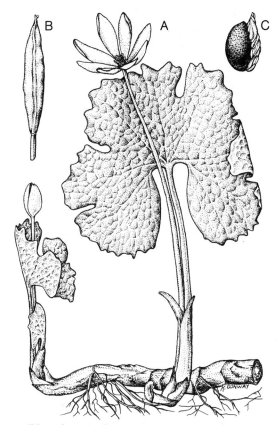

Bloodroot, Sanguinaria canadensis

A-Habit drawing B-Capsule C-Seed

d.

John W. Hatch is a professor in the Arts Department at the University of New Hampshire who specializes in water media landscape paintings of the mountains and the coast. In the summers, he is on his boat sailing the northern New England coast, filling several sketch books with drawings which contain the seeds for winter paintings.

He takes his students out a great deal to sketch directly from nature, feeling strongly that only after perceptive outdoor observation can one grow to understand how a landscape can be transcribed into a picture.

In an interview with the artist, he had the following thoughts to communicate to students when starting a landscape:

> See the landscape as a compositional whole first . . . see what is the major focus and then the various elements that relate to it. Coordinate the vertical measure with the horizontal measure. Remember the whole of the masses are worth more than the parts. You should strive to make a coherent statement.

> I'm trying to teach perception—the ability to really see. How do you see something and how do you interpret it? It may be different from the way I see it . . . that's fine as long as what you have drawn is a valid statement. You can have theory (that is, perspective) but unless you get out and look and are able to relate it to what you see, theory is useless.

> I draw to find what is essential in what I am seeing and to express how I feel about it. I believe in my sketches more than my photographs. I can see form better in my drawings. A photograph helps with color and detail, and as reference for things I might have missed. But I prefer the immediate sensation of a drawing to a photograph.

When asked what tools for sketching he uses, Hatch pulled out an old rucksack. In it contained a 12″ × 14″ drawing board with papers clipped on, a few sketchbooks, and a 12″ metal tube with a lid, containing his pens and pencils. The pens are permanent black, felt-tipped, and the pencils are the common (yellow) "Dixon" type (because they have a handy eraser on the end) and are labelled "soft" or "medium." Simplicity of field equipment, John finds, suits him best.

In an introduction to the catalogue of a show Hatch had written a statement, part of which is quoted here:

> For me, art is visual—physical and material—a form.

> > the forms in my mind are usually better than those on paper
> > but I firmly believe there is no form until the idea
> > struggles with the material which shapes that form.

> Yet I know art to be more than physical form—that it is a vehicle that speaks to the spirit and points beyond itself.

> (Addison Gallery of American Art, Andover, Mass., 1974)

Throughout several phone conversations with the renowned Canadian wildlife artist, Robert Bateman, a number of interesting points were made that, with his permission, I am including here. Bateman trained from his early years as both artist and naturalist. He said, "I knew by the time I was twelve that I was going to spend a lot of my life doing art and a lot of it looking at birds." He also said, "A great master teacher once said, 'In order to learn how to draw you have to make two thousand mistakes. Get busy and start making them.'" Today, as one of the world's leading wildlife artists, Bateman is still working constantly to express on canvas his eclectic fascination with the natural world which goes beyond the mere portrait of an animal and goes towards making the entire canvas a work of art.

a.

b.

c.

172

d.

Figure 8.13

JOHN W. HATCH

Steps toward a painting, *South Point Star II*, 1980.
a   First sketch, on site, in pencil in an 8" x 12" sketchbook.
b   Compositional study sketch done back in the studio in pencil in a 5½" x 8½"
    sketchbook.
c   Full-scale drawing in pencil on 24" x 48" tracing paper defining final
    placement of forms and color values.
d   Finished painting *South Point Star II*, 1980 by John W. Hatch, acrylic on
    gessoed masonite, 24" x 48".

John wrote an explanation regarding the series of sketches for "South Point
Star" particularly for this book and I include it here:
"My obsession with the confrontation of land, sea and sky, in what I call the
'edge experience', has led me on many occasions to embark in my boat for
sketching trips to the Isles of Shoal, ten miles off shore (from Portsmouth, New
Hampshire). One August day, I found this granite rampart on the seaward side
of Star Island and was so moved by its elemental presence that I immediately
made a pencil drawing. (See Figure 8.16A) Its full impact is best seen standing
on a precarious slippery ledge at low tide level, leaving little time for lengthy
study, therefore I concentrated on the defiant jutting jaw of this monolith.
That evening as I developed the forms from the initial sketch, it became
apparent that I needed more information about the planes of the rocks to the
left. On the second trip to the site, I drew sketches to study better the forms
describing the bulk of the rock and the island ledge. This time I took
photographs to aid in remembering light and texture.
The first preliminary compositional sketch for painting [Figure 8.16B] empha-
sized the drama of my original confrontational ideas with the bulk of rock high
to the left on a diagonal sliding into the sea with the curving line of the dike
suggesting bulk in counter movement and the sea as a thrusting wedge. After
further development of this theme it was rejected in favor of a more
presentational idea in which the rock itself became the central focus . . . Much
of this development occurred in the full scale drawing on tracing paper [Figure
8.16C] and was transferred directly to the painting panel but others, such as the
dark foreground ledge, developed in the painting process. The painting in
acrylic [Figure 8.16D] reflects my interest in resolving the inherent problems of
the textural integrity of the rock forms with the luminous character of the
bright, light fog of a summer morning."

Figure 8.14A
BRIAN PENDELTON (landscape painter from Seattle)
One of many preparatory sketches on location.

Figure 8.14B
BRIAN PENDELTON
Final oil painting of Mount Index in Washington State (22″ x 33″).

It is my sincere hope that one day the art museums will recognize the works of such wildlife artists as Robert Bateman and others like Louis Agassiz Fuertes, Frances Lee Jaques, John Busby, and Bruno Liljefors and give them the exhibition exposure that they have long deserved beside the canvases of the fine artists.

Bateman says of his work:

I have a number of things to say about sketching. I use it on several levels—one is for its own sake. I sometimes do what one might consider sketch journals and do the sketches as little completed records which do not lead to future works of art or reference. They stand or fall on their own. I also, of course, use sketches and drawings usually with little notes and arrows on them as a way of getting more information for my paintings. As I know you agree, a photograph is never enough. The other way that I use sketches is as little thumbnails that come out of my head when I am preparing compositions for my future paintings.

In sketching, you are really recording fleeting glimpses of action . . . Some of my best sketches look awful to anybody else. They look like a four-year-old's sketches. But I couldn't possibly do the posture of an animal without these sketches . . . I keep a little sketch pad with me in the car and may sketch with my right hand if there is something that catches my eye. These fleeting sketches will be part of the many sketches and resources that are used in preparing a painting . . . Much of my final

Figure 8.15—8.19B
Although Robert Bateman wishes he had more time to do field sketching on a regular basis, when he travels he takes his sketchbook with him, and it is here that he makes his travel notes. He draws sketches of people on his trip and works out ideas for new paintings. Because he travels a great deal and to a wide range of places, his subjects are broad and cover a period of many years, dating back to 1946 when he was sixteen. The five sketch pages included here represent an example of how one artist uses his sketchbook.

Figure 8.15
ROBERT BATEMAN (contemporary Canadian wildlife artist)
Wilson's Storm Petrel, Drake Passage, Antartica, 1979. Black ball-point pen.

Figure 8.16
ROBERT BATEMAN
Santa Rita, Arizona, April 10, 1982. Ball-point pen.

Figure 8.17
ROBERT BATEMEN
Phenacomys Vole, Churchill, Manitoba, 1955. Black pen and
ink over pencil.

sketching I do in paint on the canvas. Some reference sketches I did when I was between fourteen and eighteen years are still used as source material for my paintings and so are very valuable to me . . . In fact, I would say that for many artists their sketches are more valuable to them than their final paintings because it was there that the initial inspiration emerged.

What I am after [in a painting] is form, space, air, and rhythm. There are artists who can do lovely loose sketches that do not translate into paintings. You cannot get space or form in sketching. You get more posture and factual evidences. In order to get the other, you need the hours of work time in the studio.

What sorts out the amateur from the professional? The amateur does not know how to sort out, leave out, and select. Rhythmic, clear, clean, and readable is what a composition should be. Sort out different things and see subjects individually . . . Just because it is pretty, it may not make a good subject.

Although an artist's technique may change and grow throughout his life, his style of sketching often does not. Sketching is really that basic and gut response to something that, though primitive-seeming, can be the highest form of art. Many artists' best work can be seen not in their finished works but in their initial, spontaneous sketches.

Figure 8.18
ROBERT BATEMAN
View from Tokyo Hilton, Tokyo, Japan, 1980.
Black ball-point pen with pen and ink
caligraphy.

Figure 8.19A
ROBERT BATEMAN
Gentoo Penquins and Whalebones, Antartica, 1979. Black ball-point pen.

Figure 8.15—8.19B
Although Robert Bateman wishes he had more time to do field sketching on a regular basis, when he travels he takes his sketchbook with him, and it is here that he makes his travel notes. He draws sketches of people on his trip and works out ideas for new paintings. Because he travels a great deal and to a wide range of places, his subjects are broad and cover a period of many years, dating back to 1946 when he was sixteen. The five sketch pages included here represent an example of how one artist uses his sketchbook. Figure 8.19B is the final painting done several months later by Bateman once he was back in the studio.

Figure 8.19B
ROBERT BATEMAN
Painting of Gentoo Penquins and Whalebones done back in the studio, 1979.
Bateman explains that the initial sketch was done because he grew fascinated by
the sculptured forms of the whale bones with the penquins huddled down
beside, appearing miserable in their stage of molt.

Bibliography and Further Resources

This is by no means a complete list. Use it as a starting point. If some of these books seem difficult to locate, work with whatever books you can find.

TEXTS ON DRAWING AND SKETCHING

Blake, Vernon. *The Way to Sketch*. New York: Dover Publications, Inc., 1981. (Based on the 1929 edition and interesting reading.)

Blake, Wendon and Petrie, Ferdinand. *Landscape Drawing*. New York: Watson-Guptill Publications, 1981. (A helpful small paperback discussing specific topics.)

Chaet, Bernard. *The Art of Drawing*. New York: Holt, Rinehart and Winston, 1978. (One of the better books on drawing technique with good reproductions.)

Franck, Frederick. *The Zen of Seeing: Seeing/ Drawing as Meditation*. New York: Vintage Books (a division of Random House), 1973.

Franck, Frederick. *Art as a Way: A Return to the Spiritual Roots*. New York: Crossroad Publishing Company, 1981.

Gurney, James and Thomas Kincaide. *The Artist's Guide to Sketching*. New York: Watson-Guptill Publications, 1982.

Jamison, Philip. *Capturing Nature in Watercolor*. New York: Watson-Guptill Publications, 1980.

Leslie, Clare Walker. *Nature Drawing: A Tool for Learning*. Englewood Cliffs, N.J.: Prentice-Hall, Inc., 1980.

Nickolaides, Kimon. *The Natural Way to Draw*. Boston: Houghton Mifflin Company, 1941. (A classic on drawing technique.)

Petrie, Ferdinand. *Drawing Landscapes in Pencil*. New York: Watson-Guptill Publications, 1979.

FIELD GUIDES TO NATURAL HISTORY

The Audubon Society Field Guide to North American Trees. New York: Alfred A. Knopf, Inc., 1980. (Good, color photographs in paperback format.)

Borror, Donald and Richard White. *A Field Guide to the Insects of America North of Mexico*. Boston: Houghton Mifflin Company, 1970.

Burt, William H. and Richard P. Grossenheider. *A Field Guide to Mammals*. Boston: Houghton Mifflin Company, 1964. (Still a classic.)

Gosner, Kenneth L. *A Field Guide to the Atlantic Seashore*. Boston: Houghton Mifflin Company, 1978.

Palmer, E. Lawrence. *Fieldbook of Natural History*. New York: McGraw-Hill Book Company, 1974. (A concise compendium of the entire natural kingdom, valuable as a reference text.)

Peterson, Roger Tory. *A Field Guide to the Birds* (Revised edition). Boston: Houghton Mifflin Company, 1980.

Peterson, Roger Tory. *A Field Guide to Western Birds*. Boston: Houghton Mifflin Company, 1940.

Peterson, Roger Tory and Margaret McKenny. *A Field Guide to Wild Flowers (of Northeastern and North Central America)*. Boston: Houghton Mifflin Company, 1968.

Petry, Loren C. and Marcia G. Norman. *A Beachcomber's Botany*. Chatham, Mass.: The Chatham Conservation Foundation, Inc., 1963.

Rabkin, Richard and Jacob Rabkin. *Nature in the West: A Handbook of Habitats*. New York: Holt, Rinehart and Winston, 1981.

Robbins, Chandler S., Bertel Brown, and Zim Herbert. *Birds of North America*. New York: Golden Press, 1966. (Various bird guides have their loyal supporters. This is the one I prefer. Illustrated by Arthur Singer.)

Schwartz, Susan. *Nature in the Northwest*. Englewood Cliffs, N.J.: Prentice-Hall, Inc., 1983.

Silverman, Maida. *A City Herbal*. New York: Alfred A. Knopf, Inc., 1977.

Stokes, Donald W. *A Guide to the Behavior of Common Birds*. Boston: Little, Brown and Company, 1979.

Zim, Herbert and Robert Mitchell. *Butterflies and Moths*. New York: Golden Press, 1962. (Still one of the best guides in a series of small and inexpensive guides to many subjects on nature.)

BOOKS WITH REPRODUCTIONS OF FIELD SKETCHES BY GRAPHIC AND WILDLIFE ARTISTS

The Art of Beatrix Potter, with notes by Enid and Leslie Linder. London: Frederick Warne and Co., Ltd., 1955.

The Art of Robert Batemen. Toronto, Ontario: Madison Press Books, 1981. (Bateman is one of Canada's top wildlife artists today).

Duval, Paul. *The Art of Glen Loates*. Prentice-Hall Canada Inc., 1977. (A highly competent Canadian wildlife artist.)

Hoving, Thomas. *Two Worlds of Andrew Wyeth: Kuerners and Olsons*. Boston: Houghton Mifflin Company, 1977.

Kuhn, Bob. *The Animal Art of Bob Kuhn*. Westport, Conn.: Northlight Publications, a Division of Fletcher Art Services, Inc., 1973. (A well-known contemporary animal artist.)

DeJoode, Ton and Anthonie Stolk. *The Backyard Bestiary*. New York: Alfred A. Knopf, Inc., 1982. (Illustrated with fascinating pencil and watercolor drawings by the Dutch artist Kees de Kiefte, this is a good book to have for its information on local natural history.)

Lansdowne, J. Fenwick. *Birds of the West Coast*. Boston: Houghton Mifflin Company, 1976. (Lansdowne is one of the great bird painters today. The sketches in this book are worth its price.)

Leonardo da Vinci Nature Studies from the Royal Library at Windsor Castle. Catalogue by Carlo Pedretti, New York: The Metropolitan Museum of Art, 1981.

The Living Birds of Eric Ennion, with commentary by John Busby. London: Victor Gollancz, Ltd. and North Pomfret, Vermont: David and Charles, 1982. (Dr. Ennion was one of the best of the British field artist/naturalists.)

Luce, Donald T. and Laura M. Andrews. *Francis Lee Jaques: Artist-Naturalist*. Minneapolis: University of Minnesota Press, 1982. (A prominent artist naturalist during the 1940s and 1950s.)

Peck, Robert McCracken. *A Celebration of Birds: The Life and Art of Louis Agassiz Fuertes*. New York: Walker and Company, 1982. (One of America's best bird artists.)

Poortvliet, Rien. *The Living Forest*. New York: Harry N. Abrams, Inc., 1973. (Poortvliet, a Dutch artist, has observed all these animals on location and uses a most interesting sketching and painting technique.)

Scott, Peter. *Observations of Wildlife*. New York: Cornell University Press and Oxford: Phaidon Press, 1980. (Sir Peter Scott is perhaps Britain's equivalent of Roger Tory Peterson for his contribu-

tion to the public's knowledge and love of birds.)

Stebbins, Theodore E. *American Master Drawings and Watercolors*. New York: Harper & Row, Publishers, 1979. (A superb catalogue.)

Van Gelder, Patricia. *Wildlife Artists at Work*. New York: Watson-Guptill Publications, 1982.

The Work of E.H. Shepard, edited by Rawle Knox. New York: Schocken Books, 1979. (The illustrator of *Winnie the Pooh* and *Wind in the Willows* was an accomplished field sketcher.)

The Worlds of Ernest Thompson Seton. New York: Alfred A. Knopf, Inc., 1976. (Although better known as the founder of the Boy Scouts, Seton was an accomplished wildlife artist.)

PUBLISHED FIELD SKETCHBOOKS

Brockie, Keith. *Keith Brockie's Wildlife Sketchbook*. New York: MacMillan Publishing Co., Inc., 1981. (A superb example of a sketchbook using pencil with colored pencil and watercolor by a young Scottish artist.)

Brusewitz, Gunnar. *Wings and Seasons*. Stockholm, Sweden: Wahlstrom and Widstrand, 1980. (The only book of Brusewitz's illustrated sketchbooks in English.)

DeJoode, Ton and Anthonie Stolk, with illustrations by Kees De Kiefte. *The Backyard Bestiary*. New York: Alfred A. Knopf, Inc., 1982. (Pencil and watercolor illustrations with chapters on specific natural history subjects.)

Foster, Muriel C. *Muriel Foster's Fishing Diary*. New York: The Viking Press, Inc., 1980.

Holden, Edith. *The Country Diary of an Edwardian Lady*. New York: Holt,

Rinehart and Winston, 1977. (This book, perhaps more than any other, has helped awaken public interest in published field sketchbooks of plants and birds. As yet, most of these sketchbooks are British and of the Victorian or Edwardian era.)

Laing, Hamilton. *Allan Brooks: Artist/Naturalist*. Victoria, British Columbia: The British Columbia Provincial Museum, 1979.

Leslie, Clare Walker. *Notes from a Naturalist's Sketchbook*. Boston: Houghton Mifflin Company, 1981. (My own sketch journals, published at the request of Houghton Mifflin.)

Marsh, Janet. *Janet Marsh's Nature Diary*. New York: William Morrow Co., Inc., 1979. (Beautifully detailed pencil and watercolor drawings of a British river habitat.)

Thollander, Earl. *Back Roads of New England*. New York: Clarkson N. Potter, Inc., a division of Crown Publishers, Inc., 1982. (Thollander has published several of these travel guides, which are handwritten and illustrated with his own very nice pen and ink wash drawings.)

Tudor, Bethany. *Drawn From New England*. New York: Philomel Books, 1979. (A lovely book about Tasha Tudor, the well-known American illustrator of children's books.)

A Sketchbook of Birds: C. F. Tunnicliffe R. A., with introduction by Ian Niall. New York: Holt, Rinehart and Winston, 1979. (Tunnicliffe was a master and important to know about.)

Wilkinson, Gerald. *Turner's Early Sketchbooks*. New York: Watson-Guptill Publications, 1972. (J.M.W. Turner, along with many other painters of his time, kept sketchbooks containing personal field notes and observations for future paintings, which were primarily done once the artist was back in the studio.)

SOME RECOMMENDED WORKS BY NATURALIST WRITERS

Abbey, Edward. *Desert Solitaire*. New York: Ballantine Books, Inc., 1968.

Beston, Henry. *The Outermost House*. New York: The Viking Press, Inc., 1928.

Carson, Rachel. *The Edge of the Sea*. Boston: Houghton Mifflin Company, 1955.

Dillard, Annie. *Pilgrim at Tinker Creek*. New York: Harper & Row, Publishers, 1974.

Emerson, Ralph Waldo. *Selections from Ralph Waldo Emerson*. Boston: Houghton Mifflin Company, 1957.

Gibson, William Hamilton. *Sharp Eyes: A Rambler's Calendar of Fifty-Two Weeks Among Insects, Birds and Flowers*. New York: Harper & Row, Publishers, 1891. (A book that has had perhaps more influence on my study and illustration of natural history than any other.)

Haiku Harvest. Japanese Haiku Series IV, translation by Peter Beilenson and Harry Behn, Mount Vernon. New York: The Peter Pauper Press. (Any nature poetry from the Far East is advised reading as contrast to the western attitude toward nature.)

Hay, John and Peter Farb. *The Atlantic Shore*. New York: Harper & Row, Publishers, 1966.

The Heart of Thoreau's Journals, edited by Odell Shepard. New York: Dover Publications, Inc., 1927.

Krutch, Joseph Wood. *The Voice of the Desert*. New York: Morrow Quill Paperbacks, 1954.

Leopold, Aldo. *A Sand County Almanac*. New York: Oxford University Press, Inc., (A classic piece of nature writing with sketches by the author.)

The Mentor Book of Major American Poets, edited by Oscar Williams and Edwin Honig. New York: The New American Library Inc., 1962. (I recommend that you do some reading of American poets and consider their thoughts on nature.)

Teale, Edwin Way. *Circle of the Seasons*. New York: Dodd, Mead & Company, 1953. (Any of Teale's many books on nature is worth reading.)

Wallace, David Rains. *The Dark Range*. San Francisco: Sierra Club Books, 1978.

GENERAL READINGS IN NATURAL HISTORY

Fox, William, T., illustrated by Clare Walker Leslie. *At the Sea's Edge: An Introduction to Coastal Oceanography for the Amateur Naturalist*. Englewood Cliffs, N.J.: Prentice-Hall, Inc., 1983.

Jorgensen Neil. *A Sierra Club Naturalist's Guide: Northern New England and Southern New England*. San Francisco: Sierra Club Books, 1978.

Joy of Nature. Pleasantville, New York: The Reader's Digest Association, Inc., 1977. (A broad introduction to the environments of the world, with good color photographs and a clear text. Recommended for the beginning naturalist.)

Kieran, John A. *Natural History of New York City*. Boston: Houghton Mifflin Company, 1959.

Mitchell, John, and The Massachusetts Audubon Society. *The Curious Naturalist*. Englewood Cliffs, N.J.: Prentice-Hall, Inc., 1980.

Roth, Charles E. *The Wildlife Observer's Guidebook*. Englewood Cliffs, N.J.: Prentice-Hall, Inc., 1982.

Smith, Robert L. *Ecology and Field Biology*. New York: Harper & Row, Publishers, 1966. (An excellent text for the college biology student.)

Stokes, Donald W. Publishers. *A Guide to Nature in Winter*. Boston: Little, Brown and Company, 1976.

RESOURCES FOR NATURAL HISTORY STUDY

Investigate your local Chamber of Commerce, nature centers, zoos, town conservation commissions, and the bulletin board of the town library or town hall. Inquire about courses at adult education centers or adult extension programs at local schools or college biology departments. Spend time browsing in local libraries, bookstores, art and science museums, and magazine racks that may have some of the current nature and outdoor recreation magazines. Remember a study of natural history is largely going to be a self-directed course.

American Conservation Association, 30 Rockefeller Plaza, Room 5425, New York, New York 10020.

Audubon Naturalist Society of the Central Atlantic States, 8940 Jones Mill Road, Washington, D.C. 20015.

College of the Atlantic, Bar Harbor, Maine 04609.

Defenders of Wildlife, 1244 19th Street N.E., Washington, D.C. 20036.

Ducks Unlimited, P.O. Box 66300, Chicago, Illinois 60666.

Earthwatch, Research Expeditions, Box 127, Belmont, Massachusetts 02178.

National Audubon Society, 950 Third Avenue, New York, New York 10022.

National Outdoor Leadership School, Box AA, Lander, Wyoming 82520.

National Wildlife Federation, 1412 Sixteenth Street N.W., Washington, D.C. 20036.

Nature Canada Federation, 46 Elgin Street, Ottawa KIP5K6, Canada.

Orion Nature Quarterly, published quarterly by The Myrin Institute, Inc., 136 East 6th Street, New York, New York 10021. (A review of current books and thoughts on natural history.)

Sierra Club, Chapter Services, 530 Bush Street, San Francisco, California 94108.

Index

Index

Hudson River school, 46
Hunting Scene (Gainsborough), 41

I

Identification sketches, 91–92
Ingres, Jean, 18

J

Jacques, Francis Lee, 86, 124, 175
Johnson, Cathy, 56, 118
Johnston, Alan, 56

K

Karpetian, Paul, 76
Kieran, John, 104
Kuhn, Bob, 101

L

Lakes, 138–39
Landscapes, 36–46, 97, 120, 145–48, 171–73
La Salle, New York, August 18, 1892 (Walker), 138
Leslie, Clare Walker, 3, 72, 86, 87, 109–10, 133, 143, 147, 151
Light, 36, 42, 44
Liljefors, Bruno, 175
Lindell, Steve, 60, 85, 90, 111–12, 153
Linear perspective, 41
Lorrain, Claude, 34

M

Magnifying glass, 10
Mariedel, April 14, 1978 (Brusewitz), 42
Marshes, 138, 142–43
Mass, 36, 44
McQueen, Larry, 15, 128
Meadows, 109–10
Measures, David, 155
Meditation, drawing as, 21–22
Memory sketch, 17, 79
Merrick, Beth D., 162
Messick, Lyla R., 59, 143
Michelangelo, 18
Middleground, 37, 38
Mountains, 123–25

Mounts, 26, 125–26
Murie, Olaus, 161

N

National Museum of Natural History, Washington, D.C., 104
Natural History of New York City, A (Kieran), 104
Nature study, 27, 56
Negative space, 24
Notes from a Naturalist's Sketchbook (Leslie), 48, 49

O

Observation, 17, 94

P

Page layout, 22
Papers, 1, 3–4, 23
Pebble Beach, Monhegan Island, Maine (Hart), 151
Pencil line, experimenting with, 20
Pencils, 4, 5, 7
Pencil sharpeners, 5
Pendleton, Brian, 174
Pens, 5–7
Perspective, 36, 41–43
Peterson, Roger Tory, 11, 17, 19, 26
Photographs, 10–11, 25–26, 44, 125
Picasso, Pablo, 18
Planes, 38
Plastic bags, 11
Ponds, 138–39
Potter, Beatrix, 8
Powzyk, Joyce A., 165
Prairies, 109
Preliminary study, field sketching as, 159–79
Prince, Deborah, 24, 140
Proportions, 23–24

Q

Quick gesture sketch, 18–19, 87

R

Rembrandt van Rijn, 18, 46, 120
River valleys, 118